Milford's Memoir

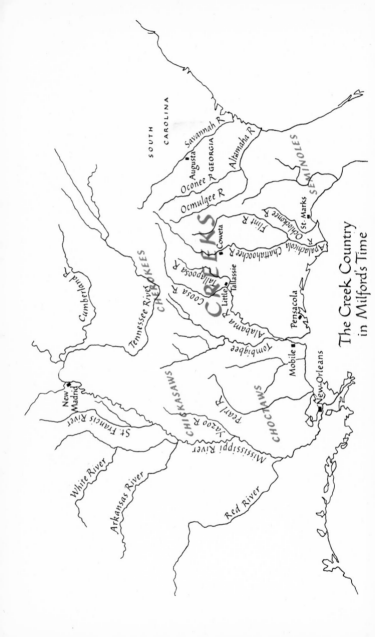

The Creek Country in Milford's Time

𝔗𝔥𝔢 𝔏𝔞𝔨𝔢𝔰𝔦𝔡𝔢 ℭ𝔩𝔞𝔰𝔰𝔦𝔠𝔰

MEMOIR

or

A Cursory Glance at My Different Travels & My Sojourn in the Creek Nation

By Louis LeClerc de Milford

Translated by
GERALDINE DE COURCY

Edited by
JOHN FRANCIS McDERMOTT

𝔗𝔥𝔢 𝔏𝔞𝔨𝔢𝔰𝔦𝔡𝔢 ℑ𝔯𝔢𝔰𝔰

R. R. DONNELLEY & SONS COMPANY

CHICAGO

Christmas, 1956

PUBLISHERS' PREFACE

ALTHOUGH it has been stated on several occasions that the Publishers of the Lakeside Classics are not committed to "continuity of subject matter, either as to time or place," the selections during the past forty years or more have fallen into the category of *Western* Americana. The volume this year represents a departure from this pattern in several respects.

There have been a number of instances where we reprinted a translation of the original publication and in one instance a translation was used that had not been published but was ready to hand. But this is the first volume of the Classics for which a translation was made after the narrative had been selected. Miss De Courcy has found it possible to carry out a difficult assignment. Not only has she provided a proper translation but she has been able to carry into the English text the charm of the original. We are grateful to her for her interest and for the result. She worked from a copy of the original edition of 1802 for the loan of which we are again indebted to The Newberry Library.

Another major change is in the scene of the story. For some years the Publishers have been considering material having to do with what is

now the southeastern part of the United States.
Their selection of *Milford's Memoir* was enthusi-
astically endorsed by several devotees of Americana who believed that it deserved a wider reading than was possible with no edition in English
available. Milford has provided us with a tale
that we believe will hold the interest of our
readers. It reflects an intimate knowledge of the
Indians, their way of life and their manner of
carrying on warfare as well as their relations with
the English, Americans, French and Spaniards
who were competing for the trade with the natives over whose territory they were trying to
gain control.

In his "Important Notice to the Reader" the
author has called attention to inaccuracies in his
statements and the reason for his not taking time
to correct them. To bring these into proper focus
has been the task of the editor who has used both
the footnotes and the historical introduction to
correct the inaccuracies and otherwise provide
necessary background. Instead of following the
customary procedure and turning to Dr. Quaife
who has so ably edited the Classics for the past
forty years, the Publishers this year turned to
Mr. John Francis McDermott of the faculty of
Washington University who has specialized in
the history of the Mississippi Valley and the territory adjacent to it. To him we are indebted

for the thoroughness with which he completed his task.

Again the Company has had a most successful year. Demands for its services by its customers, old and new, continue to grow. To meet these more effectively in one special area, land was acquired and a plant built this year in Willard, Ohio.

As our business has grown, and printing facilities have grown in intricacy and cost, it has become increasingly difficult to finance new facilities without additional capital investment. Present plans for expansion based on anticipated needs of present and future customers involve considerable capital expenditure over the next several years. Accordingly, in June for the first time in its ninety-two year history, the Company made an offering of stock to the public. The ready acceptance of the offer by investors has been gratifying as an expression of confidence, and the directors and officers of the Company are determined to do all in their power to justify it.

Again we send our best wishes for the Christmas holidays and a happy New Year.

THE PUBLISHERS

Christmas, 1956

CONTENTS

xv

PART II

Contents   xvii

CHAPTER   PAGE

HISTORICAL INTRODUCTION

THE "impulsiveness of youth" sent Louis de Milford early in 1775 wandering from France first to Norway and then to America. Landing in New London, Connecticut, in April, he traveled through the thirteen colonies for more than a year. Curiosity about reputed man-eating Indians (who could be no worse, he thought, than backwoods Americans) led him from the Carolinas into Creek country. There in May, 1776, he met Alexander McGillivray, "Beloved Man" of one of the Creek towns, and went to live with him at Little Tallassie on the Coosa River near its junction with the Tallapoosa.

Milford now sought military service with his new friends—who after all had no desire to eat him. Permitted to go on a "campaign" with the "army" (the terms are his), he made a name for himself and was accepted as a warrior. Soon he rose to Little War Chief and within three or four years he was made Tastanegy or Grand War Chief for all the towns of the Creek Confederacy. As commander-in-chief of all Creek forces in time of war, head of a military potential of five or six thousand men, Milford had reached a peak of glory. But he refused to accept this high office until his friend McGillivray was made Grand Chief of the Creek nation.

The French having joined the Americans in the Revolution, Milford decided to go traveling in order to avoid leading the Creeks (allied to the English) against his own people. He invited two hundred young warriors to go on a jaunt with him to find the caves near the headwaters of the Red River where, the old men of the tribe had told him, the Creeks had originated. This tour of the west, based solely on curiosity, without stimulus of plunder or war-glory, lasted for eighteen months. No dissension, no disciplinary problems, no commissary or *materiel* difficulties marred the exploration. At the caves they captured five hundred wild horses which they drove northwards over the plains until they reached the Missouri and then over prairie and through forest to arrive home at last, after more than sixty-five hundred miles of travel, with their horses laden with peltry. All this was simply accomplished.

Milford's story after that was one triumph after another. He urged the formation of a confederacy of *all* the American tribes in the struggle against the United States. He led a successful war against Georgia (little did the Americans know it was a Frenchman leading the victorious Indians). He drove out the scoundrelly adventurer Bowles when that Anglo-American attempted to wrest control of the Creek nation from McGillivray and Milford. He refused to let President George Washington bribe him with a general's commission and pay. By the time McGillivray died in 1793 Milford was so completely the great man of the Creeks that he succeeded his friend both as head of the nation and as commissioner of the Spanish government. Only when Spain declared war on France did he feel obliged to resign and ask for his passports to go home.[1]

For some time he had been meditating silently what service he could render his native country. He now called together his Indian brothers-in-arms who had a thousand times seen him brave death at their head and he spoke of their ancient friends the French, whose character so well sympathized with theirs. He told them it was possible to have the French for neighbors once more. This idea was received with transport by all the assembled chiefs of the Creek nation, who charged him to go to France as their representative. Though a thousand dangers menaced him, he set out in an English vessel for Philadelphia. In the

[1]Thus far the summary is from Milford's book, here translated for the first time. The remainder of his story is gathered from his Mémoire Présenté par François Tastanegy, Grand Chef de Guerre de la Nation Crik. Au Directoire Exécutif de la République française. En l'an Cinq (Archives Nationales, AF IV, 1211) and other papers cited in the next several notes.

American capital he met Citizen Fauchet, Minister Plenipotentiary of the French Republic, who commended him for his zeal and urged him to lay his plans before the home officials.

He crossed the Atlantic and, presenting himself before the Committee of Public Safety, urged the importance of France's taking possession of Louisiana and the Floridas to block the advance of the Americans, who otherwise would soon sweep everything before them. Progress was slow. The months passed and Milford still awaited action. Peace had first to be made with Spain, he was told, but that peace was presently made without the retrocession of Louisiana. Undiscouraged, the ambassador from the Creeks undertook to prove the possibility of developing a French colony in the neighborhood of the Spanish possessions. His ascendancy over the Indians, the known love that the French had had for their fathers, the protection that would be promised them, all assured to France an immense territory and formidable power. But the difficult circumstances in which the Committee found itself did not permit consideration of so distant a project, however glowingly presented. With the establishment of the new constitution Milford addressed the Minister of Foreign Relations, who gave him encouragement and presented him to the Directory, which in turn conferred on him the grade of Brigadier-General to console and sustain him while awaiting the moment to put his zeal and his special knowledge to the proof.

In the year V (1796-1797) he submitted to the Directory over the signature François Tastanegy a lengthy paper on the necessity of a French establishment in continental North America and on the part he himself could play in bringing this about. He set forth the many advantages of the project as well as the ease with which it could be accomplished. "This immense territory that I am charged to offer you and to join to Louisiana, this garden of the world that can be shared by all the French who will come to people and cultivate it" was worth the having, he urged. As ambassador, he was likewise charged by his Indian brothers to offer their arms and to contract an alliance, offensive and defensive. This support was not at all to be disdained, he declared, as the United States had more than once experienced proof of Creek valor. The Americans would long remember the defeat of their General Clark, so acclaimed for understanding the tactics to use against the Indians, this General Clark who with ten thousand regulars had been defeated by the Tastanegy with six thousand Indians of the Northern Tribes at Detroit, a victory all the more remarkable because Milford had had to employ twenty interpreters to make his plan of battle understood by the many different tribes he had brought together for the combat.

Impressive and alluring as Milford made his proposal, many months passed without action. In the Year VII he resubmitted his memoir.[2] On the 11th Vendémiaire (2 October 1798) it was sent by the Directory to the Minister of Foreign Relations and recommended for his examination. To Milford that minister wrote politely a week later: "The Executive Directory, Citizen, has sent me your memoir on North America: I have read it with pleasure and in it I have found matter worthy of the most serious attention. I will submit it to the Directory."[3]

Again silence. Not until almost two years later (17 Thermidor, an VIII—5 August 1800) is there further official word. A statement by Milford that Spain had improperly ceded a part of Louisiana to the United States interested Bonaparte as possibly being useful in any negotiations over the return of Louisiana to France. A week later, however, the First Consul was informed that there was no basis in fact for Milford's assertion: he had misunderstood or had been ignorant of the provisions of the treaty of 1783—Spain had

[2]François Tastaneegy Grand Chef de Guerre de la Nation Crik Aux Membres du Directoire Executif de la Republique française (Ministère des Affaires Étrangères, États-Unis, 50: 236).

[3]Affaires Étrangères, États-Unis, 50: 262.

merely given in at last to the demands of the
United States and acknowledged that the northern boundary of West Florida was the 31st parallel.[4]

Milford did not give up. The ceding of Louisiana to France in 1800 encouraged him to battle
on. After all, he was seeking to be the French
representative in a Creek-French state. In July,
1802, he was battling with the *Gazette de France*.[5]
In the middle of August he wrote excitedly to the
Minister of Marine that he had just been assured
"in the most positive manner" that the Ambassador of the United States had the day before sent
to the First Consul a memoir discussing the possibility of selling Louisiana to the United States.
This paper, he said, had been drawn up in a
number of copies for distribution to persons fa-
voring the proposition. To save the First Consul
from being surprised in this negotiation Milford
asked to see the memoir so that he could send the
minister his observations on an arrangement
which, he was persuaded, would be sadly disastrous for France whatever the price offered.[6]

[4]Affaires Étrangères, États-Unis, sup. 7: 138; 52: 235.
[5]Colonies, C 13 A, 51: 224 (to the Minister); 51: 226
(draft of letter to editor); and *Gazette de France*, 10 Thermidor, year 10 (reprint: pp. 1241–1242).
[6]Colonies, C 13 A, 51: 55. The memoir to which Milford referred was probably that sent by Robert Livingston
to the Secretary of State, Paris, 10 August 1802 (*State*

Perhaps his opinion was not sought. While discussions continued with the United States, the preparations for the reoccupation of Louisiana went forward. General Victor was to sail in November. Milford was driven to extreme measures. In a final attempt to bring to the attention of Bonaparte and the world his knowledge of the Creek country, his influence with the Creeks, and the international significance of his plans, he wrote "at top speed" his *Mémoire ou Coup-d'oeil Rapide sur mes Différens Voyages et mon Séjour dans la Nation Crëck.* "My sole object in describing my travels," he declared in the preface, "has

Papers Bearing upon the Louisiana Purchase, 36–50). That Milford had made an impression at least on the American negotiators is evident from an earlier letter from Livingston to the Secretary (Paris, 24 March 1802): the French, he wrote, "are made to believe this is one of the most fertile and important countries in the world; that they have a much greater interest with the Indians than any other people; that New Orleans must command the trade of our whole Western country; and, of course, that they will have a leading interest in its politics. It is a darling object with the First Consul, who sees in it a means to gratify his friends, and to dispose of his armies. There is a man here, who calls himself a Frenchman, by the name of Francis Tatergem, who pretends to have great interest with the Creek nations. He has been advanced to the rank of General of Division. He persuades them that the Indians are extremely attached to France, and hate the Americans; that they can raise 20,000 warriors; that the country is a paradise, etc. I believe him to be a mere adventurer; but he is listened to, and was first taken up by the old Directors" (*Ibid.,* 20).

been to let the French Government know that my
sojourn among the Indians and the position I
held in the Creek nation have, perforce, placed
me in a position to be of service to it in any expeditions that it may be contemplating on the continent of North America." The book was rushed
into print probably early in the year XI (fall of
1802), but his hopes for a place in General Victor's expedition came to nothing, for it never left
port. And to nothing finally came all his plans
when on 30 April 1803 Bonaparte signed the bill
of sale to the United States.

* * *

Such is Milford's story as he set it forth in his
printed *Mémoire* and in papers addressed to the
French government. That some of his claims and
statements of fact are open to doubt is immediately apparent. It is true that he wrote the
Mémoire under pressure years after the event,
from memory, without notes, without benefit of
books or maps, without editorial advice, without
even the time to reread the manuscript before it
went to the printer. He admitted that his narrative had faults of style and that the chronological
order was "often confused," and he hoped later
to present his ideas "in a more polished style."
But his eagerness to establish his own importance
in the eyes of French officials, as well as his haste,

led him frequently into inaccuracies and over-statement.

A simple attempt to trace on the map Milford's journey to the Red River caves makes clear that he was not to be relied on as geographer or topographer. His assertions that he held together for eighteen months a party of two hundred young warriors and that for more than a year they drove a herd of five hundred horses over thousands of miles until they reached home in Alabama without loss of a man must strike readers as something new in Indian customs and behavior.

Milford stated that he settled in the Creek country in May, 1776, that he was made Tastanegy of the entire nation in 1780, that at the same time McGillivray was made Head Chief. None of the considerable file of documents available for the Creeks, however, mentions Milford before 1788, though it is possible that he was living there as early as 1785. McGillivray, though important enough among the Creeks to have been made a colonel and an agent by the English during the Revolutionary War, was clearly not the head of the entire nation before 1783 at the earliest. And, though every town had its Tastanegy or head warrior, there was none for the entire nation at the early date Milford gives. Furthermore, it appears certain that in 1776 McGillivray had but recently returned to the tribe from South Carolina and was then only seventeen years old, so that in 1780 he was still very young to be taking over control of the Creek Confederacy.[7]

On setting out for the Red River caves in February, 1781, Milford declared that he visited Mobile and made the acquaintance of Pierre Favrot, the commandant. But he could not have done so, for Favrot at that time was commanding at Baton Rouge on the Mississippi. It was not until 28 June 1784 that he assumed command at Mobile, and it was possibly in that year or the next that Milford first met him. Milford reported that the Acadians settled at New Madrid in 1785. He gave *Viegaz* as the name of the commandant at the Spanish fort of San Marcos in 1792 whereas Vegas did not command there until two years later. The Creek treaty with Spain (1784) was not made at Mobile but at Pensacola. The Creek-Georgian war did not take place immediately after the close of the Revolution and the making of the Creek-Spanish treaty but in 1787–1788. Milford was never offered either commission or salary by Washington in 1790. He confused the

[7]Alexander McGillivray (1759?–1793), son of Lachlan McGillivray, was one-half Scottish, one-quarter French, and one-quarter Creek, a brilliant leader in a losing cause. The fullest accounts of his career are Caughey, *McGillivray of the Creeks*, 3–57 and Whitaker, "Alexander McGillivray, 1783–1793."

Sicoto land scandals with the attempt to grab the Yazoo lands. He was not Spanish commissary to the Creeks in the sense that McGillivray had been and he was not paid annually the sum of thirty-five hundred piastres for his services.

* * *

Even in the face of these discrepancies and distortions (the list could be enlarged) let us not be in haste to brand Milford a "hopeless liar."[8] Rather let us say that he gave free rein to his imagination and his enthusiasm. He had undertaken to sell the French government on an "embassy" to the Creek nation and an alliance with it—with a good place for himself right in the middle. If he blew himself up somewhat larger than life, we ought not to be surprised. He did live among the Creeks for ten years, if not for the twenty he asserted. He was a man of some minor importance, if not the imposing military figure and influential adviser he pictured himself. His share in Creek history can be established from records other than his own, and, if he does not show to grand advantage, his part is not without honor and usefulness.

Louis LeClerc de Milford was born near midcentury at Tirles-Moutiers, a village near Mézières,

[8] So Turner called him in the *American Historical Review,* X, 271.

in Ardennes. Later in life he asserted that it had
been his misfortune in killing in a duel a member
of the king's household that led him to take
refuge in America.[9] It is more than doubtful,
however, that he arrived in the Creek country in
1776, for nothing in his own narrative substan-
tiates the claim and a reliable witness, Enrique
White, an officer in the fixed regiment of Louisiana and presently acting governor at Pensacola,
placed him there no earlier than 1785.[10]

Milford began to play a part of record at the
time of the first Bowles "invasion" of the Creek
country in 1788. In this affair McGillivray, as
head chief of the nation, desirous of strengthen-
ing his people however possible, was ready to
find what advantage he could. The influences behind Bowles were not at first apparent. The firm
of Miller and Bonamy of Providence in the Bahamas, backed by Lord Dunmore, the governor,
determined to cut in on the profitable Creek
trade of Panton, Leslie and Company. For their
agent they picked William Augustus Bowles because for several years in the latter part of the
war he had lived among the Creeks and knew

[9]Michaud, *Biographie Universelle*, XXVIII, 288. Michaud followed the publisher in printing his name *Milfort*. Since, however, he invariably signed his letters *Milford*, I have followed his style.

[10]White to Miró, 1792, cited by Whitaker, "Alexander
McGillivray," 182, n.8.

their language and their ways. The young man
went to the lower Creek towns ostensibly with a
gift of powder and ball from a charitable society
in England that had heard of distress among the
Creeks. "He gave me great hopes of Succour &
aid, beside many other fine things that wore
rather an Improbable face," McGillivray wrote to
John Leslie in some uncertainty of mind on 20
November 1788. "I questioned him a good deal
about who engaged him in the enterprise, but he
wouldn't Satisfy me at this time. but pointedly
denied that D[unmore] was any ways concernd.
After landing his arms & ammn. he was to return
with fresh Instructions, before this time, but has
not yet appeared. Come when he will he will be
exposed before the Indians & dismissed for a
Needy Vagrant."[11]

In December Bowles returned with more goods.
McGillivray met him again, and again questioned
him about his supporters. "He produced papers
which convinced me that an abundant and effective help and aid was destined for me." However,
McGillivray's suspicions were increasing. When
Bowles proposed to go to the mouth of the Flint
to meet the ship and bring the promised goods
by river, McGillivray "agreed to the proposition
and proposed to my Frenchman ... to accompany him in order to keep off impertinent In-

[11]Caughey, *McGillivray of the Creeks,* 205.

dians." He charged Milford "very particularly to use the greatest skill, in order to learn from Bowles or Richmond, the treasurer of Bonamy, (towards whom I knew he had the sharpest animosity because he treated him as a domestic) every material circumstance relative to the nature and true object of his visits, etc." Milford, Bowles, and Richmond went down to the mouth of the Flint and waited from 25 December until "into January." Bowles now lost patience and decided to return to his friends at one of the lower towns, but "the Frenchman proposed that he and Richmond wait another two weeks with the Indians." Bowles agreed and left.[12]

"Meanwhile," continued McGillivray, "Richmond and the Frenchman Milfortt were together. Richmond spoke of Bowles without reserve. The Frenchman learned from him that Bowles had frequently visited Miller's house because he was known by his brother, boasting of his former experiences in the Indian country and among other things insinuating that Panton and Company enjoyed an interesting trade in the Floridas, and that nothing could be easier than to supplant them and take this trade away from them, and that he was sure he could do it by his own in-

[12]The statements in this paragraph and the next are from McGillivray to Leslie, Little Tallassie, 8 February 1789 (Caughey, *McGillivray of the Creeks*, 222–223).

fluence if the execution was left to him. And in order more surely to wrest this trade from its present monopolist, he proposed to offer, or better to subject me to the necessity of opening a port in one of the many channels or bays with which the coast abounds, and that he must attract by presents the people of the continent to join me, and that, in short, he would acquire such a number that the project would inevitably succeed." McGillivray added thoughtfully, "It seems to me that his backers have chosen an instrument not at all appropriate for such undertakings . . . he does not seem to be suited to great things."

On 1 February 1789 Milford returned to Little Tallassie with his packet of news, confirming McGillivray's suspicions. The Bowles ship at last arrived, bearing some munitions but nothing more, and the ambitious adventurer found it advisable to leave the nation. Without trade goods he could make little headway. McGillivray was content to be rid of him: "Your Excellencys humanity," he wrote to Miró at New Orleans, "does not require his blood to be shed in this Country, but I will assure you that he shall be compelld to leave this nation never to return to it."[13]

[13]McGillivray to Panton, Little Tallassie, 1 February 1789; to Miró, 1 February 1789 (Caughey, *McGillivray of the Creeks,* 218–219.

We hear of Milford again on the breaking up in May, 1789, of the annual "Convention of the lower Towns," which eleven Cherokee chiefs had attended. "Agreeable to the Resolution" taken to attack the Georgians on the disputed Ogeechee, "Numbers are turning out every where," McGillivray wrote Panton from Little Tallassie on the 20th. "I have again given the Mareschall's Staff to Milford who sett out yesterday to join a Large party."[14] The campaign, however, cannot have been a long one, for in June McGillivray sent him to Pensacola to see to the delivery of some arms and ammunition.[15]

During the next few years we catch an occasional glimpse of Milford. A man named Romain, who had come into the Creek country in the summer of 1789 with a scheme to buy negroes to sell in New Orleans, "had a difference with Milfort, who threatened to Send him in Irons to Orleans, which terrified him Apparently, and he went off to the Cherokees."[16] No doubt Milford was present at the abortive treaty meeting at Rock Landing in September of this year, for McGillivray had "nine hundred chosen men"

[14]Corbitt, "Papers Relating to the Georgia-Florida Frontier," XXI, 286–287.

[15]McGillivray to Cruzat, Little Tallassie, 2 July 1789 (Caughey, *McGillivray of the Creeks,* 241).

[16]McGillivray to Panton, Little Tallassie, 15 August 1789 (Caughey, *McGillivray of the Creeks,* 249).

there, but the Frenchman's name did not get into any of the records.[17] The following May, McGillivray sent him on business to Pensacola where he managed to stir up some kind of trouble. "Knowing something of his rashness of temper I always Strictly Charged him to Conduct himself in a Manner that Might not give any room for Censure either on his own account or mine, & on which subject I have been very free with him," the Head Chief assured Governor O'Neill, "he Shall no more be in any Situation which Shall give Your Excellency any future umbrage."[18]

In September, 1791, the curtain rose on the second act of the Bowles drama. According to the well-informed William Panton, that young man had had many adventures since he had last been seen in the Floridas:

His History from the time of his being drove from the Nation in the winter of 1789, is somewhat extraordinary, and is a proof of his enterprise and perseverance. When he went off he had address enough to prevail on two three half Breeds of the cherokess & a Couple of Young fellows from the Creeks to accompany him to New Providence where he was soon after his arrival put in jail for debt; But having got out of Confinement from the influence of Lord Dunmore he with his Indians escaped over to the Florida Point,

[17]Caughey, *McGillivray of the Creeks*, 254.
[18]Little Tallassie, 2 November 1790 (Caughey, *McGillivray of the Creeks*, 286).

where it is said the Indians had resolved to kill him, and would have done it for the deception he had practiced on them, if accident had not preserved him by throwing a Spanish vessel ashore near where he and his Indians were encamped. The crew of the vessel & passengers having left the wreck Bowles and his people took possession of Her wherin they found a Considerable booty, and among other things some suits of very Rich Gold laced Clothes with which he equiped his party and having hired a fishing Boat that happened to be there catching Turtle he proceeded to Nova Scotia where he introduced his Indians & himself to Govr. Parr as Men of the first rank & Consequence of the Creek & Cherokee Nations. And So artfully did he Conduct himself, that the Governor listned to his Storry and believed it. From Nova Scotia he was Sent on to Lord Dorchester, the Governor Genl. of Canada, and from thence he was Conducted to England, and was Carressed and entertained at the Public expense. I am pretty certain that Mr. Pitt was not ignorant of Bowles's being an Imposture, Yet, it suited his purpose during the dispute with Spain, and he was passed upon the Spanish Ambassadore as a Man of the greatest Consequence among the Southern Indians. After these disputes were settled the minister packed him & his Party out to America. It is Said they were accompanied with handsome presents but to what amount I know not.[19]

Bowles, having returned to the West Indies, managed to slip into the Creek country with a

[19]Panton to Miró, Pensacola, 8 October 1791 (Caughey, *McGillivray of the Creeks,* 296–297).

commission from the English Secretary of State appointing him Superintendent and General, and he assured the Indians that he came to rescue them from Panton and McGillivray and the Americans. His main design obviously was to supplant Panton in the Indian trade. McGillivray sent "three Warriors to dispatch the Vagabond," but they returned unsuccessful because he was well guarded by some of his Indian friends.[20] In January, 1792, to demonstrate to his Indians what he could do, Bowles seized the Panton, Leslie house at San Marcos on the Apalachee. He made no move against the Spanish fort there, but the commandant in turn was too weak to take any counter action. A few weeks later, Bowles was "Inticed to an Interview & seized by the Commandant at St. Marks."[21] Taken under safe conduct to New Orleans, he spent years in Spanish prisons until his escape and his third incursion in 1800.

Before his capture, however, he had caused considerable alarm, and Milford had been called into action. It is not exactly true that Bowles begged the commandant of Fort San Marcos to protect him from the Frenchman, but the latter

[20]McGillivray to Panton, Little Tallassie, 28 October 1791 (Caughey, *McGillivray of the Creeks,* 298–299).

[21]McGillivray to Panton, Little Tallassie, 27 March 1792 (Corbitt, "Papers Relating to the Georgia-Florida Frontier," XXII, 191).

was indeed "on his trail." A full report of Milford's usefulness in this affair was made by Panton to Carondelet:

On the 2d of this month our schooner returned from Appalachy with Mr. Milford on board—Your Excellency will remember that I sent this Person to the lower Towns with my talk, and to head and lead down to the Appalachy, as many of the Indians, who, in consequence of the Robbery Committed at that place had become willing to go against Bowles—He left this the 20th February and on the 5th of March he arrived at the lower Towns,—on the 6th he delivered my talk to the Indians and on the 10th of March the Indians had got their provisions prepared and to the number of about 140 began their March, the day after he was joined by two hundred and fifty more, and on the 14th he had advanced down the Banks of the Flint River to James Burgesses house within two days march of Appalachy.

There he received the first certain account of the Capture of Bowles, but not withstanding they had lost their chief, a couple hundred of the plundering Indians were still held together by some of Bowles White Bandittie, and were still encamped near the mouth of Occalagany—To lessen the expense as much as possible, he discharged most of his Indians, and went on to the Camps of the Robbing party, who after much hesitation, and a long parley between the leaders of the opposite partys, the Robbers were at last dispersed—As Milford will be the bearer himself of this letter I must refer you to him for a more particular detail of this expedition which altho' too late to come at Bowles was not the less meritorious, and was at last of great service; because it dispersed those plunderers, who were still in a Body sufficient to Commit mischief and who were only waiting for the expiration of the forty days allowed for Bowles return, to Sett about taking satisfaction for his Capture.[22]

Further recognition of Milford's services came in a very practical form. Robert Leslie at Apalachee told Panton to "pay Mr. Milford Five Hundred Dollars as a gratuity from the house, for his alacrity and promptness in Coming to my assistance, [I assure] you that the manner in which he bestirred & exerted himself in this affair reflects a high Credit upon him."[23]

Milford's story must have lost nothing in the re-telling to the Governor at New Orleans, but it is clear that he did not make quite the impression he expected. "My intention never was to employ Milfort except in expeditions which require more handwork than headwork," the Baron wrote McGillivray.

"He fancied that I allowed him five hundred dollars from the day of his arrival in town. In truth I promised him that sum in case he should be useful on an occasion to be indicated later, but his arrogance toward Don Pedro

[22]Pensacola, 12 April 1792 (Corbitt, "Papers Relating to the Georgia-Florida Frontier," XXII, 289-290).

[23]Corbitt, "Papers Relating to the Georgia-Florida Frontier," XXII, 291).

Olivier to whom he is by no means obedient, according to information from Governor O Neill, though Olivier is commissioned Royal Commissary of His Majesty in the Creek Nation, displeased me exceedingly and dissuaded me from employing him in the future."[24] Nevertheless, the Baron must have changed his mind, for it is clear that Milford was on the Spanish payroll from the first of May, 1792, until his departure for France.[25]

Olivier was to become Milford's chief thorn. He had been appointed by Carondelet early in February, 1792, to live among the Creeks to "support the credit & authority" of McGillivray and to assist in opposing Bowles. Settled at Little Tallassie, he soon began to feel the animosity of Milfort, for the latter did not like to see another white man being used officially.[26] He found Olivier's "presence in the Nation unpleasant," Carondelet told McGillivray, and "hopes that he may succeed to the employ of King's Commissary." The two got on badly, Milford endeavoring

[24]New Orleans, 14 September 1792 (Caughey, *McGillivray of the Creeks*, 338).

[25]Milford to Carondelet, Tuquetbachet, 26 May 1793; Enrique White to Carondelet, Pensacola, 4 July 1793; Las Casas to Campo de Alange, 19 May 1794 (Kinnaird, *Spain in the Mississippi Valley*, III, 162, 178, 288).

[26]Caughey, *McGillivray of the Creeks*, 307, 313, 326, 327.

to create misunderstanding between Olivier and McGillivray.[27]

Relations between the Tastanegy and the Head Chief now became somewhat strained. It is possible that they quarreled and that Milford separated from his wife, McGillivray's sister. By the spring of 1793 the Frenchman had moved from his Little Paris plantation to the Tuka-bachee town. "McGilvrit and I feared each other. I feared him because I knew his spirit and the malice of his family, and he feared me because he knew how strong my influence was, being general of the nation and always ready to march at their head whenever it was necessary," he declared to Carondelet.[28] But if he feared McGillivray and broke with him, he was also able to say that McGillivray's death had caused him "baucoupt de paine."[29]

Whatever their relations, on the death of Mc-Gillivray Milford thought to step into his place. He was even ready to work with Olivier if that would win the support of Carondelet. We find him in May, 1793, in the capacity of head chief recalling the twelve hundred men sent out

[27]New Orleans, 22 October 1792 (Caughey, *McGillivray of the Creeks,* 342).
[28]Tuquetbachet, 26 May 1793 (Caughey, *McGillivray of the Creeks,* 358–359).
[29]Milford to Carondelet, 29 March 1793, cited in Whitaker, "Alexander McGillivray," 307.

against the Chickasaws as soon as word reached him from O'Neill that peace negotiations were under way. He reported to Carondelet, too, that he had moved to Tukabachee because "the chiefs required it of me" and that he decided to hold a general conference of the Creeks on June 5.[30]

But the hope of getting along with Olivier was not bright. That official did not believe Milford would make the grade.

These Indians do not show themselves at all disposed to advance Mr. Milford to the office or title which McGillivray held among them. I have heard that he has written to Your Lordship that they had already elected him, but this never existed anywhere except in his head. This was the cause of some debates between him and me, during which I have been under the necessity of telling him Your Lordship's intentions in this matter and my way of thinking, in order to make him understand the independence which the commissioners of His Majesty ought to preserve in this nation. It seems that he believed that he was already authorized to conduct himself as a little soverign. This came to the attention of the Indians, and I believe was the reason why they expressed themselves plainly to me in the assembly, telling me clearly that they respected Mr. Milford as a man who had lived among them many years and who had been employed by McGillivray on some commissions with the Indians in which he merited the title or name of

[30]Milford to O'Neill, Tuquebachet, 31 April 1793; Milford to Carondelet, Tuquet Bachet, 26 May 1793 (Kinnaird, *Spain in the Mississippi Valley,* III, 154, 160–162).

Tostanaky, which signifies warrior. They said that
they regarded him in that light, and would allow him
to remain among them as long as he wished. They
stated that they had been told that he was employed
by the government, which was very good, and, if
Your Lordship desired to give him a commission,
they would attend to whatever he told them con-
ducive to the good of the nation. This was an
allusion to the order which he holds from Your
Lordship to arrest the agent of the Americans and
send him as a prisoner to some one of our posts.
They have not liked the order at all, and I greatly
doubt that they would permit it to be carried out if
anyone should attempt it.[31]

Although Milford did not succeed to the pres-
tige and power of McGillivray, he continued for a
time to act as agent for Spain to some portion of
the Creek nation and, in fact, actually outlasted
his hated rival Olivier. Sometimes he met difficulties cleverly. On one occasion when Olivier
was absent from his post Milford received orders
from the governor to send down the head of an
Indian who had killed a white man. Realizing the
awkwardness of his situation, he decided to let
the man carry his own head to the capital. He
sent down the offender with a note: "You have
demanded the head of the Indian who murdered
the man above Natches; the bearer is the man;
I have sent him to you, head and all."[32]

[31]Olivier to Carondelet, Mongulacha, 11 June 1793
(Kinnaird, *Spain in the Mississippi Valley,* III, 170–171).
[32]Hawkins, *Letters,* 247.

In the spring of 1794 Milford was in temporary charge after the transfer of Olivier and before the arrival of his successor. He seems to have been busy. "I have had lots of trouble trying to quiet down the Indians," he wrote to Carondelet on April 14. "However, it seems to me that I have partly succeeded in preventing the Upper Creeks from disturbing your province. . . . A great number of Lower Creeks have just left to rob and kill the people in the vicinity of St. Augustine. I have worn out my horses trying to save your province from the same peril and this is the reason I cannot go myself to call them back. Although I have twelve horses for my ordinary purposes, I do not have one at present which is capable of two days' travel."[33]

But for all the earnestness of his effort Milford could not manage the Creeks as McGillivray had done. Difficulties with his immediate superiors, with American agents, and with his Indian and half-breed associates proved too much for his skill. The last we hear of him is in a statement by White Lieutenant, a Creek chief, who wrote to Carondelet, 14 November 1794, that "Mr. Millford, and the man you sent last to us they are no Body & their hearts & Tongues are not straight there is now no beloved man of yours amongest us."[34] Just when Milford parted from the Creeks

[33]Kinnaird, *Spain in the Mississippi Valley,* III, 266–268.
[34]Kinnaird, *Spain in the Mississippi Valley,* III, 377.

we do not know. Let us take his word that he left the nation in 1795, met Fauchet in Philadelphia before August in that year, and then sailed to lay before the French government his plans for the redemption of Louisiana.

After the collapse of his hopes following the sale of Louisiana Milford gave up thought of returning to America. Possibly he settled in his native corner of France. Nothing is known of his later life save that on the invasion of 1814 he was placed in command of a volunteer company at Mézières because of his experience in Indian fighting. His mission was to cut the communications of the enemy and in general to harass him, but it is said that he caused more unquiet to the Ardennais than to the invader, and his force was soon disbanded. After this very brief campaign he left Mézières for Vouziers where he fortified his house and beat off an attack by Uhlans during the second invasion. Immediately after this victorious private action, however, he returned to Mézières where he died in 1817, leaving a wife and an infant.[35]   *   *   *

Milford's book did not accomplish its primary purpose of getting its author a job but it has preserved his name in the literature of travel. If he found no fortune as an administrator, he did

[35]Michaud, *Biographie Universelle*, XXVIII, 288–289.

win a spot of fame as a writer, for his odd little story is filled with tales and details of interest and value.

There is a certain charm about the naive way this young man wandered through a strange land gathering such impressions as he was able. "The crimes to which the spirit of faction" between the Whigs and Tories on the frontier gave rise, the behavior of the Crackers or Gougers in the Carolina backcountry, led him to doubt that there were any wickeder people on earth than these "Anglo-Americans." The report of savage tribes in the interior who ate every European they could lay hands on made so extraordinary a picture to him that he had to see them, whatever the risk. So the innocent fellow bought himself a traveler's compass "to be always sure of going in the right direction." As we follow his uncertain footsteps, we must wonder if he had not been sold a "wooden nutmeg." For more than thirty days he rode alone through the forests west from the Savannah River until at last he reached the town of Coweta two hundred miles away on the Chattahoochee. And even from that moment when he was received among the Creeks until, at the close of the book, he recounted the display of male prowess that led to his marriage with McGillivray's sister, there is an air of the boy about all he says.

But the book does not rest on an unwitting humor in its personal narrative. Having the good fortune to fall in with Alexander McGillivray, a great man among the Creeks, Milford was not long in finding a place of importance among them. He discovered that his friend was no mere savage but lived in real comfort, owning some fifty or sixty slaves, and he himself was presently set up in a nearby village where he maintained the residence which he called Little Paris. There he lived for years among the Creeks in a position to observe and report their ways.

Now he shows us a typical town square with its places of honor arranged in precise recognition of rank and leads us into the council house where the principal chiefs of all the towns in the confederacy meet every spring to deliberate on the affairs of the nation. We see the dignity with which the Creeks welcome a newcomer to residence in their country. We watch them making the black drink and are, with Milford, surprised and shocked at the manner of partaking of it, but this is a custom of the country and must be shared in by anyone who wishes a place in Creek life. We are amused by the coquetry of a Creek girl dressed in the height of Indian fashion. We have a glimpse of the celebration of the Busk or Festival of New Fires in August when the Indians for the first time eat the new grain of the season out of new dishes and forget and forgive their enmities—the new year is to begin new in all ways.

Milford finds his place in the Creek world by becoming a soldier. The ceremonies for the installation of a tastanegy or "Big Warrior," the significance of the war medicine in the successful outcome of a campaign, the nature of the war discipline, the manner of taking a scalp, the importance of the scalp as trophy and the importance of success in war to obtain rank in Creek society—these are reported in effective detail. Milford's affairs lead him into frequent contact with the Choctaws. He describes their care of the sick, their medicine men as doctors, their burial customs, their feasts of horseflesh, their habits as beggars, and their punishment of wives taken in adultery. These are but a few of many lively passages in a book which in effect pictures the Indians standing precariously between the Franco-Spanish colonial systems and the rapidly expanding United States.

However egotistical and opinionated Milford was, however ready to twist any fact or situation to his advantage in his eagerness for a job, his *Mémoire* remains an entertaining and useful book filled with curious lore and observations.

Milford's *Mémoire,* never reprinted after its original publication in 1802, is here translated for the first time. Miss de Courcy's able rendering of a frequently obscure and difficult text now makes it available to the general reader. In the editing I have accumulated debts which I am happy to acknowledge. Professor Marcel Giraud of the Collège de France was kind enough to obtain from the archives in Paris documents which enabled me to trace something of Milford's activities after his return home. The University of Florida, the University of Michigan, and the Newberry Libraries supplied me with microfilms of otherwise unavailable books about the South in Milford's day. My own Washington University Library and the St. Louis Mercantile Library have been forebearing in my extended use of their collections, and I am particularly obliged to my friend Mr. Clarence E. Miller, librarian of the Mercantile, for very special courtesies. Most of all I am conscious beyond words of the never-ceasing help of Mary Stephanie McDermott, my wife, for her critical reading as well as for her patient services as typist and indexer.

JOHN FRANCIS MCDERMOTT

Washington University
March, 1956

MÉMOIRE

OU

COUP-D'ŒIL RAPIDE

SUR mes différens voyages et mon séjour
dans la nation Crëck.

PAR LE G^{AL}. MILFORT,

*Tastanégy ou grand Chef de guerre de la
nation Crëck, et Général de brigade au service
de la République francaise.*

A PARIS,

DE L'IMPRIMERIE DE GIGUET ET MICHAUD,
RUE DES BONS-ENFANS, N°. 6.

AN XI. — (1802.)

To Bonaparte

General-Consul:

I have the honor to offer you a little work entitled: *A Cursory Glance at my Travels among the Savage Tribes of North America*. The haste in which it has been written, the imperfection that inevitably results from such precipitation, have made me hesitate to present it to you; but it seemed to me that this work belongs to you for the reason that it treats of a part of the world where the glory of your name is already widely disseminated, and particularly because it has to do with a brave, good people worthy of forming an alliance with the French and who have sent me here for the express purpose of cementing such a union. It is in the name of this same people, General-Consul, that I take the liberty of proffering it to you. Positive of their deep gratitude, should you vouchsafe to accept the homage, I do not hesitate to assure you that they will regard this graciousness on your part as evidence of your good intentions towards them. Flattered at being their present advocate with you, I seize this fortunate conjuncture to profess to you my unbounded devotion and to assure you of the profound respect with which I am, General-Consul,

Your very obedient servant,

MILFORT

Tastanegy or Grand War Chief of the Creek Nation

Important Notice to the Reader

IN giving the public a summary of my various travels among the savage tribes of North America, I did not presume to think the work would represent a valuable contribution to the history of the world. I know too well the complexities of the subject and my own deficiencies to aspire to such a great distinction; I had even less intention to write a romance, and I assure the reader that I have been a spectator, and oftener still an actor, in the events reported here, or they were related to me by the chiefs of the nation that I have the honor to command. He will find their language too simple and too artless to believe them capable of dissimulation. I present the facts and incidents narrated to me all the more confidently in that I have been able to verify the greater part of them. To a practiced writer, this slight essay would furnish ample materials for a long history; but, having passed twenty years of my youth amid forests and among men still in a primitive state, and having almost totally forgotten the French language through the necessity of speaking exclusively a foreign tongue and oftentimes a horrible jargon, I have had to content myself with stating the facts as concisely and competently as possible. My first demand of the reader is his unbounded indulgence. I beg him not to dwell upon the imperfections, even the faults of style, which he can encounter at every stride, and not to lose sight of the fact that my sole object in describing my travels has been to let the French Government know that my long sojourn among the Indians and the position I held in the Creek nation have, perforce, placed me in a position to be of service to it in any expeditions that it may be contemplating on the continent of North America.

Further, I must inform the reader that this work has been written at top speed, that is, in about three weeks; that I have written it from memory, and without notes. In consequence, the chronological order is often confused. Special considerations compelled me to divide my account into two parts and to extract from their subordinate or accessory events the more important matters in order to throw the essential into greater relief. Such a division calls for long, sustained work, which I was unable to devote to it. The urgency of the Louisiana Expedition, which is about to be carried out, has even prevented my going back over it. I am giving it to the printer just as it is, with the intention later of correcting, and even amplifying, it considerably if the public deigns to receive it favorably, bearing in mind only the motives that prompted it, which I shall set forth in a more highly polished work.

PART I

Milford's Memoir

PART I

DEPARTURE FROM FRANCE AND ARRIVAL
AMONG THE CREEKS

THERE are few, if any, exact accounts of the savage nations that inhabit North America.[1] The relations that the Europeans have had with these tribes have always been too slight for them to get to know the habits, the usages, and the way of life of these Indians. The character of barbarians attributed to them terrified those who might have desired to go amongst them; all intercourse was limited to barter commerce on the frontiers. Chance and, I must confess, the impulsiveness of youth having afforded me this advantage, which has been enjoyed by few, I thought the public might be grateful for a detailed account of my travels over the vast spaces

[1]Other valuable accounts of the southern Indians about this time include: Bossu, *Nouveaux Voyages aux Indes Occidentales* (Paris, 1768); Adair, *History of the American Indians* (London, 1775); Romans, *A Concise Natural History of East and West Florida* (New York, 1775); Bartram, *Travels* (Philadelphia, 1791); Hutchins, *An Historical Narrative and Topographical Description of Louisiana, and West-Florida* (Philadelphia, 1784).

of this continent. I regret that the circumstances under which I am writing do not permit me to devote to it all the care and time that such a work demands. I shall content myself with relating succinctly the more interesting things. If I were writing the history of my life, I should begin with my early childhood; but I am writing only the history of my travels and shall therefore commence with the moment I left France, to be absent for a period of twenty years.

DEPARTURE FROM FRANCE

In the course of January, 1775, I found at Dunkerque a vessel bound for Norway, and my main idea being to travel in the north of Europe, I took advantage of this opportunity. When I arrived in Bergen, I found there another ship, this one on the point of sailing for the United States of America, which gave me the idea of going there. Since travel was my object and I had no definite goal, the direction was wholly immaterial to me. I therefore embarked on this vessel and disembarked at New London, Connecticut, in April that same year. From this town, of which I shall speak more fully in Part II of this work, along with all the others I passed through on my way to the Creeks, I went to Norwich, then to Providence and Newport and from there to Boston. On this journey, near sixty leagues in length, I found nothing worthy of remark except the antipathy existing between the inhabitants of the North and the South.[2]

ARRIVAL IN THE UNITED STATES

I stopped several days in Boston to refresh myself and then proceeded to New York, going from there to Jersey [*sic*], situated on the Delaware River, which flows under the walls of Philadelphia. I left Jersey and passed through Philadelphia on my way to Baltimore; from there I went to Yorktown in Virginia (where Lord Cornwallis was [later] taken prisoner by the united French and American forces); from Yorktown I traversed the two Carolinas and arrived at Savannah, Georgia. This region, which now is densely populated, was then very sparsely settled. I shall give the reason for this in Part II.[3] From Savannah I proceeded north again on the river of that name as far as Augusta, today an important town but at that time only a small village.[4] From there

[2] In Part II (p. 128) he lays this antipathy to the "religion of the Quakers" which forbade negro slavery and therefore made the Northerners envious of the Southerners who profited by slave labor!

[3] All the dishonest vagrants and outlaws produced by the war were in 1784 driven into Georgia by the honest citizens of the Carolinas, Milford says (pp. 130–131).

[4] William Bartram in 1773 found the buildings of Augusta spread out for nearly two miles along the Savannah River (*Travels*, 32).

I went to Orangeburg on the outskirts of South Carolina.[5] I left that town and went due east ten leagues on the road to Tugaloo, where I was surprised to find a fairly large quantity of vines cultivated as they are in France. I learned that a native of Bordeaux, a former Knight of St. Louis who, having met with misfortunes and disgrace in France, had decided to emigrate to the West Indies with his family and had settled in this part of the new world. This man was M. de St. Pierre. His name and the aforesaid circumstances should be known in Bordeaux. Being French he had no difficulty in obtaining from the Shawnee Indians inhabiting this region the land on which he planted the vines, but the wine he produces, and which I tasted, is no better than the very poorest quality of French wine.[6]

[5]Orangeburg, South Carolina, was about sixty miles due *east* of Augusta.

[6]Milford is writing from memory and, apparently, without a map to draw on. To go to Tugaloo he must have returned to the Savannah and proceeded upstream about one hundred and twenty-five miles to the northwest. Bartram (1777) "lodged at the farm of Mons. St. Pierre, a French gentleman, who received and entertained us with great politeness and hospitality. The mansion-house is situated on the top of a very high hill near the banks of the river Savanna, overlooking his very extensive and well cultivated plantations of Indian Corn (Zea) Rice, Wheat, Oats, Indigo, Convolvulus Batata, &c. these are rich low lands, lying very level betwixt these natural heights and the river; his gardens occupy the gentle descent on one

In wandering through the backwoods of the United States, I visited Tugaloo, Franklin and other places inhabited by a peculiar class of Anglo-Americans called Gougers. They were all one-eyed, the reason for which I shall explain in Part II.[7] I [had] then traveled through the thirteen colonies of the United States, which now number sixteen owing to the addition of Kentucky and Cumberland.[8] Here I encountered only hatred and animosity. These people are divided into two parties, which are constantly at daggers drawn. One of them is called Whig and the other Tory. The crimes to which this spirit of faction daily gives rise made me doubt whether there are wickeder people on earth. I told them this and they replied that back of the United States, if one penetrates one hundred to one hundred and fifty leagues into the interior, one finds savage tribes barbarous enough to torture a man to death and to eat all the Europeans they can lay their hands on.

They drew—what seemed to me—so extraordinary a picture of these people that it made

side of the mount, and a very thriving vineyard, consisting of about five acres, is on the other side." This plantation Bartram located about twenty miles above the junction of the Broad and Savannah Rivers (*Travels*, 373).

[7]P. 132. He apparently means the Blue Ridge country near the Georgia-North Carolina border.

[8]Vermont, 1790; Kentucky, 1792; Tennessee, 1796.

me want to go and see them even at the risk of being roasted and eaten. My repugnance for these Anglo-Americans greatly diminished in my eyes the perils of such a journey. Moreover, the desire to see these savages and the country, both of which were apparently quite unknown, decided me forthwith. In order to be able to reach these man-eaters, or cannibals, of whose real character one knew next to nothing and of whose geographical location one could only give me a general idea, I bought myself a traveler's compass so as to be always sure of going in the right direction. At the same time I acquired three horses, one for myself, a second for my servant, and a third to carry the equipment and provisions.

DEPARTURE FROM THE UNITED STATES

I then set out from the vicinage of Tugaloo and plunged into an immense forest where no trail had been marked out.[9] At the end of two days march, my servant, who was a German, informed me that he was not inclined to follow me any farther and requested leave to turn back. I gave him some provisions and continued on my way alone. I confess that the journey then seemed far

[9]Ignorant of the country and without map or guide Milford quickly lost his way. The road he should have taken is described by Bartram (*Travels*, 374 ff.). For a full account of it see Goff, "The Path to Oakfuskee: Upper Trading Route in Georgia to the Creek Indians."

more arduous to me, yet I was none the less determined to go on with it. I proceeded in the same direction, always hoping to run across some tribe. I continued thus for the space of a fortnight, sleeping in the forest and living from my provisions, which at the end of this time were totally exhausted.

This did not worry me too much because in the vast forests that lay in my path, I found a great many fruit-bearing trees. I admit, however, that when I saw myself reduced to eating these wild fruits and acorns, I began to feel some regrets at having thus ventured to undertake an enterprise without any definite goal and with no knowledge of the country through which I was traveling. Nevertheless, I felt that I had gone too far to turn back, and each day therefore made it more and more impossible for me to retrace my steps. Ready for anything that might befall me, I kept on for another fortnight, which proved very strenuous and exhausting, since I had to swim my horses across several rivers, such as the Big and Little Oconee, the Altamaha and some other smaller streams. At the end of this time I came to a river called by the English *Flint River*, or the River of Flintstones. Worn out with hunger and fatigue and not knowing whether I was near some settlement or whether they were still some distance off, I stopped on the banks of the river for several hours to rest. After eating a little of my bad food, I set off again and proceeded another forty leagues [*sic*], stopping near a beautiful spring where I gave myself over to my thoughts, which were by no means gay or reassuring.[10] I had very violent pains in my stomach —for a fortnight I had eaten nothing but wild fruits and acorns—which brought home to me the necessity of taking more substantial food. This I could only procure by hunting, but it was impossible for me to avail myself of this facility because I had only sufficient supplies of this nature for my personal safety, and furthermore I could not leave my horses, which I should never have been able to find again. In short, I think that in the course of human existence there are few situations more frightful than the one in which I then found myself. All things considered, I decided to kill one of my horses for food and was just preparing to do so when I heard a

[10]It is not possible to chart Milford's wanderings. Whether he was traveling southwest from the Tugaloo settlements or west from Augusta, he did not cross the Altamaha, since that name applied only to the stream formed by the Oconee and the Ocmulgee; he may have used Altamaha for the latter river. His measures of distance seem exaggerated: unless he walked constantly in circles it would have been impossible for him to travel forty leagues (one hundred miles) from the time he crossed the Flint until he met the first Creek Indian at a point one hour east of the Chattahoochee.

noise quite near me. I was looking round to see from whence it came when I caught sight of two savages, two women, and a negro of about twelve years. If they were not as gratified to see me as I to see them, it was not difficult to perceive that they were just as surprised as I, and since I was armed with a rifle, they did not dare approach me. I grounded it and made signs to them that reassured them. The first to come towards me was an old man whose venerable appearance and the respect the others showed him made me think that he might be their father—as in fact he proved to be. He spoke to me in his native tongue, which I did not understand, but I gathered from his gesticulations that he was asking me whence I came and who I was. In replying I mentioned the word *French* and to my unutterable satisfaction I noted that this word was not unknown to him, for he immediately came towards me, and smiling, held out his hand.[11] Although I did not have the faintest notion what he intended to do with me, the position in which I found myself was too distressing to permit of any reflections on my part; for I knew no danger greater than the hunger that tormented me. I

[11]"My friendly reception and the old man's visible pleasure in hearing the word *French* will not be surprising when one learns that the Grand Medal had been conferred upon him by the Governor of Louisiana when that territory was French."—Milford.

therefore placed myself entirely in their hands, resolved to do everything they demanded of me. The old man made a lengthy speech that I did not understand but which seemed to give great pleasure to the two women and the savage who were with him. The latter taking charge of my two horses and equipment, we set off in a westerly direction, when all at once, at a signal from the old man, the young negro ran off with astonishing swiftness. Then the old man asked me by signs what I was planning to do with the rifle I had in my hand when he first espied me. I explained to him that driven by hunger, I was about to kill one of my horses for food. He then pointed to the sun and traced a short line with his finger to indicate that by the time that luminary should have traversed this short distance, we would be at his house.

ARRIVAL AMONG THE CREEKS

After about an hour's march—which seemed an age to me, I was so ravenously hungry—we came to the bank of a river called the Chattahoochie on the other side of which lay the town of Coweta.[12] It was here that my guide lived. The

[12]In the neighborhood of present day Phenix City, Alabama, opposite Columbus, Georgia. The Cowetas were one of the principal towns in the Creek Confederacy. Swanton, *Early History of the Creek Indians*, 225–230.

young negro who had run on ahead had received orders to get the canoes ready for our passage. We also found him waiting for us with several companions. When we arrived at the old man's house, he had me sit down and offered me a pipe of tobacco and a light. Although this did not seem to me to be the most pressing occupation in my existing situation, I none the less took the pipe and smoked it, which did me a world of good. When I had finished, he offered me a slice of watermelon, he likewise eating some; but he did not wish me to have any more. Judging from the way I gulped it down, he felt that if left to my own devices, I should surely make myself ill. So I had to content myself with that small portion.

Whilst we were eating our melon, I heard a drum a short distance away. Noting my evident surprise, he gave me to understand that they were about to hold an assembly and offered to escort me there. As I understood nothing that he said to me, I made up my mind to do everything he wished. The hospitable manner in which he had received me had dissipated all my fears; and though his garments seemed to me extraordinary, I doubted whether I had already arrived among one of the savage tribes where I should be roasted and eaten. Nevertheless, my arrival in the Creek nation, where I remained

twenty years and of which I have become the
Grand War Chief, as will be seen from the following account, dates from this time, that is,
from May, 1776, seventeen months after my departure from France; for this man was one of the
elders of the Creek nation.

Counting from the time I left the Anglo-
Americans up to my arrival in the town of
Coweta, I had traveled thirty-two days. Although
a distance of only one hundred leagues, I had
gone much farther owing to my ignorance of the
proper route. I arrived just at the time the chiefs
of the nation were wont to convene their annual
national council.[13] When the assembly opened,
my host informed them that he had a Frenchman
with him and, since the business in hand had not
yet begun, they decided to receive me, and the
old man was asked to bring me there.[14] He came
indeed to fetch me and escorted me to the assembly where he presented me to a man seated on a
bearskin in the center, whom I took to be the
chief. He was not so dark in color as the others
and was not much older than I. He motioned to

[13]Bossu (1759) noted that the Creeks held an annual
council of the nation in the principal town (*Nouveaux
Voyages*, IJ, 54). Milford will later describe such a council
in detail—see p. 143 ff.
[14]"Although my host was not a chief, he could enter
the Grand Cabin of the Assembly in his capacity of elder."
—Milford.

me to sit down alongside him on the same bearskin and shook hands with me in token of friendship. I said some words to him in French, but
seeing that he did not understand me, I spoke
broken English to him, which he understood at
once since he spoke the language perfectly. This
man, in short, was Alexander McGillivray, who
has been mentioned so often in the North American, and even the English, papers. Although at
that time he was only *isti àtcagàgi*, that is,
Beloved Man, he had come to this town to preside
at the grand council.[15]

[15]"McGillivray was not made Supreme Chief till I was
appointed Grand War Chief."—Milford. There seems to
be an inconsistency here. McGillivray would hardly have
been presiding over the grand council of the nation in his
capacity of Beloved Man of one town. If Milford is correct
in dating his own arrival among the Creeks 1776, McGillivray was then only seventeen years old. It is far more
likely that the Frenchman met him some years later when
he had become head chief in fact if not in name. Milford's
unreliability in dates is discussed in the editor's introduction. Before the outbreak of the Revolution and the
proscription of his father, young McGillivray had spent
two years at school in Charleston. The *isti àtcagàgi* were
generally chosen from the elders of a town; that McGillivray was so recognized as a young man must have been
owing to the esteem that his father had won among the
Creeks, to the wealth that the son had inherited, and to
the fact that through his mother he belonged to the
powerful Wind clan, as well as to his quickly demon-
strated ability. (For a discussion of this rank of Beloved
Man see Swanton, "Social Organization of the Creek Confederacy," 301–305).

Since as a foreigner, I was not permitted to remain at the assembly, my host came to get me to take me back to his house. On arrival there he gave me a glass of rum, which I drank, and he then served me an excellent meal to which I did full credit because I had not had anything like it for a long time. As I could only understand his sign language, he was thoughtful enough to invite McGillivray to have dinner with us, and the latter then served as my interpreter. I spoke English well enough to make myself understood, which was very agreeable for McGillivray who spoke very little Indian.[16] During dinner we had a long conversation in which I told him that it was my intention to stop in the nation for some time at least. He thereupon expressed a wish to have me join him; he even wanted me to go at once to the friends with whom he was stopping, but he feared lest the old man who had extended me hospitality should take offense. We therefore agreed that as soon as the council was over, I should remain in the town of Coweta only long enough to rest and then we should both leave and go to his plantation. As for my horses and equipment, I could leave them with the old man who would look after them and bring them to me

[16]In Part II I shall explain why he did not speak the native language very well, though he was Beloved Man." —Milford.

when the horses were sufficiently rested; in fact, he would be very glad to have this opportunity of visiting his chief.

I was very flattered at McGillivray's offer and very inclined to accept it, but at the same time I was tormented by the fear that my departure would distress my host to whom I was so greatly indebted. I told McGillivray what was passing in my mind and he took it upon himself to arrange matters with the good old man and to assure him of my deep gratitude. A week after the closure of the grand council, feeling completely recovered from my fatigue, I notified McGillivray that I was prepared to go with him whenever he thought fit to leave. We made ready for our journey and set out at once. I confess that I left with great regret a house that had been my first refuge when I was destitute of everything. I said good-by to my host and made him promise to come to see me very soon at the Beloved Man's. He kept his word, and six months later paid me his first visit, which he then repeated every year. He was with me when I left for France and exacted a promise from me not to be away long so that he could embrace me once again before he died.

DEPARTURE FROM COWETA

McGillivray and I set out and after four days march arrived at a village called Little Tallassie, or Village of the Hickory Trees. McGillivray's house is near this village on the banks of Coosa River, half a league from Fort Toulouse, which formerly belonged to the French and is now the site of the village of Taskigi (Tuskegee). This habitation seemed very beautiful to me; McGillivray had sixty negroes in his service, each of whom had a cabin of his own, which gave his plantation the air of a little village.[17]

[17]John Pope (June, 1791) located McGillivray's house "on the *Cousee* River, about 5 miles above its Junction with the *Tallipoosee*" and "his upper Plantation, on the same River, about 6 Miles distant from his present Residence: Thither I impaired in Company with his Nephew . . . where the General was superintending some Workmen in the Erection of a Log House embellished with dormer Windows, on the very Spot where his Father resided whilst a Trader in the Nation. Here are some tall old Apple-trees planted by his Father, which make a venerable Appearance, tho' greatly obstruct the Prospect to and from his rural Palace . . . . He has a considerable Number of Negroes at his different Plantations, probably more than Fifty, and common Report says, double that Number in the Spanish West-India Islands; as also large Stocks of Horses, Hogs, and horned Cattle. Two or three White Men superintend their respective Ranges, and now and then collect them together in Order to brand, mark, &c: . . . His Table smokes with good substantial Diet, and his Side-board displays a Variety of Wines and ardent Spirits" (*Tour*, 46–49). The Tuskegee village on the site of Fort Toulouse near the junction of the Coosa and Tallapoosa Rivers (a few miles north of Montgomery) and Otciapofa (the Hickory Ground) or Little Tallassie were described in some detail by Hawkins as he found them in 1798 (*Sketch*, 37–40).

Sketch of Little Tallassie, or the Hickory Ground

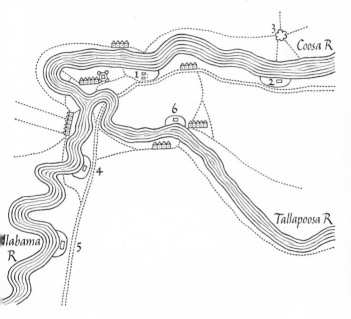

☝ Indian Towns
☘ Old French fort Alabama
.... Indian paths

▪ 1 M'Gillivray's plantation   4 Chs. Weatherford's place
□ 2 M'Gillivray's apple-grove   5 M'Gillivray's sister's place
    3 M'Gillivray's cow-pen   6 Milford's place

From Swan, "State of the Creek Nation in 1791"

I SETTLE IN THE CREEK NATION

During our journey McGillivray did all he could to persuade me to settle in the Creek nation; he described to me their docile, kindly ways and their fine reputation, and completely effaced the bad impression given me by the Anglo-Americans. He said that if I decided to stay he hoped that I would not leave him and to that end he would give me a dwelling with him where I should be absolutely my own master. Such a kind reception made it impossible for me to refuse. Moreover, we had conceived for one another such a high regard that it would already have been painful to us both to separate.

One will not be surprised at such a rapid intimacy when one learns that McGillivray, though born amongst savages, was far from being one himself and was very intelligent and well-educated. His father, who was a Scotchman, had taught him only English so that he spoke very little of the language of the people among whom he lived and of whom he had become one of the chiefs. The reason the Creek language was difficult for him was that this nation is an aggregation of ten to twelve different tribes, as I shall explain in Part II, all of which have preserved their own languages.[18] As a result, it was a real satisfaction

[18]See pp. 183–188.

to him to associate with a man with whom he could have friendly social relations and converse of the manners and customs of the people of Europe, of whom he knew very little.

As for myself, I was in duty bound, through gratitude, to comply with the wishes of a man who, with singularly rare frankness and disinterestedness, offered to share his possessions with me. Besides, I found such a marked difference between the way of life of these people called savages and that of the Anglo-Americans, who call themselves civilized, that I was constrained, in spite of myself, to accept McGillivray's offer.

Therefore on May 15, 1776, I took up my residence on his premises,[19] which his friendship soon made me look upon as my own. I had not been settled long before an occasion presented itself to give McGillivray, as well as the Creek nation, proof of my gratitude and my entire devotion to their interests.

I SERVE AS SOLDIER

I was informed that secret preparations were being made for a hostile expedition, and I asked to be allowed to serve as private soldier. My re-

[19]Enrique White, acting governor of Pensacola, in 1792 wrote to Governor Miró of Louisiana that Milford had been among the Creeks only seven years (Whitaker, "Alexander McGillivray," p. 182, n. 8).

quest, though very flattering to McGillivray, was nevertheless refused. They said that I had been too short a time among them for me to be given the honor of defending the nation, that other occasions might arise where my services would be acceptable. I appreciated the prudence of this rejection, and it increased my desire to eradicate every vestige of doubt regarding my sentiments. I reiterated my request and obtained the solicited favor, though not without some difficulty. I even learned later that, had I not been French, I should not have been accepted in the army. McGillivray's friendship and my repeated entreaties finally led to my being accepted as a soldier.[20]

The army set out, and I quickly noticed that several subordinate chiefs, under the pretext of friendship, had been charged to keep an eye on me. When we were at close quarters with the enemy, they did not let me out of their sight. When the chiefs convened the council of war to draw up a plan of operations, my being an European inspired them with a desire to learn my ideas in this respect. They summoned me to the assembly and asked my advice. At first I declined to give it, alleging that I was ignorant of their customs and their manner of making war as well as those of the enemy we were going to fight. They begged me so urgently that I finally

[20]For more about war customs see pp. 153–154, 165–177.

consented. Since at that time they made war only by surprise and by night and never in pitched battle—at least if not forced to do so by the enemy—I proposed to them a plan much more in conformity with European tactics, which being totally unknown to the enemy, was eminently successful. This war gave me the opportunity of showing my zeal and courage in several battles. The certainty that I was being watched, my French nationality for which I saw that these tribes had great veneration, the reputation of courage acquired by the French when they were masters of this part of the continent, were powerful incentives for me; and I declare without vanity that I sustained the high opinion they had formed of my countrymen. However, I must here confess with equal candor that in my first engagement with these savages I was so horrified by their method of fighting and their manner of painting their body that only the powerful stimulus of being French kept me from being terror-stricken. I can assure the reader that the different colors with which they paint all over their totally naked bodies make them more frightful than the devils in the ballets at the opera. When the campaign was over, though it was of slight importance, my companions in arms as well as the chiefs overwhelmed me with eulogies and manifested great interest in me. The very eagerness of the chiefs to recall to my mind the advice I had given them in the war council showed me that I had already made a long stride towards meriting their confidence. The praise they bestowed upon me on our return was extremely pleasing to McGillivray, who hailed me as one of the saviours of the country.[21] He told me that I should often have occasion to give renewed proof of my courage and zeal in serving the nation, because the Anglo-Americans and certain Indian tribes made frequent incursions into Creek territory.

I was not long, in fact, in finding a new opportunity of enhancing my credit and reputation.

[21]"I have traveled through a large part of Europe and nowhere have I found men so grateful and so generous as these savages generally are."—Milford. "Saviour of the country" is a grandiloquent way of saying that Milford had proved himself as a warrior and now had some standing in the tribe. "When the young warrior, after a successful expedition, approaches the town he belongs to, he announces his arrival by the war-hoop, which can be heard a mile or more, and his friends go out to meet him. The scalp he has taken is then suspended on the end of a red painted wand, and, amidst the yelling multitude, accompanied with the war-song, is brought in triumph by him into the square, or centre of the town, where it is either deposited, or cut up and divided among his friends, who then dub him *a man and a warrior*, worthy of a *war-name*, and a seat at the ceremony of the black-drink, which he receives accordingly" (Swan, "State of the Creek Nation," 280). Hawkins said that "all who go to war, and are in company, when a scalp is taken, get a war name. The leader reports their conduct, and they receive a name accordingly" (*Sketch*, 70).

There was a second expedition, and I was readily accepted as a volunteer. I was quite happy to be able to render a very great service to the army, which had rashly embarked on an engagement and had made dispositions that proved of great advantage to the enemy. It was not without exposing myself to very grave danger that I succeeded in altering this mischievous disposition and in saving a portion of the army that most certainly would have been destroyed.

I AM APPOINTED LITTLE WAR CHIEF

On returning from this expedition, the war chiefs, no longer doubting the purity of my intentions, reported to the council of elders the services I had rendered to the army, services that they indeed exaggerated even as they did the dangers I had braved. At the same time, they proposed making me Little War Chief, without troops. This title, which flattered the vanity of McGillivray—my declared protector—as much as it did mine, was unanimously conferred on me at the end of two years sojourn in the nation.[22]

[22]Milford had apparently been advanced to the second class of warriors, the top class being the *tàstànàgi*, with a "Great Leader" or "Big Warrior," selected by the *mico* (chief or king) and the *isti àtcagàgi*, placed over all in the town. See Hawkins, *Sketch*, 70. Much of Swanton's lengthy discussion is drawn from Milford ("Social Organization of the Creek Confederacy," 297–301).

This gave me a distinguished rank among the warriors, and I only wanted a chance to justify in the eyes of the chiefs the confidence of which they had given me such gratifying testimony. The following year afforded me this opportunity. The young warriors were mustered for an important expedition. I reported under the title granted me on my return from the last campaign, and I left with the army. When we were in the proximity of the enemy, the chiefs called their council together to draw up a plan of campaign.[23]

My rank of Little War Chief entitled me to be present, and there I gave them some advice that was greatly appreciated; whereupon the Band Chiefs, to whom I proposed new tactics, decided that, in order to carry out my suggested plans, I should take over the command of the army for this one campaign. It was my third year in the nation, and I had given so many proofs of my devotion to its interests that I was looked upon as a native, eligible for all kinds of posts. I accepted all the more willingly the position offered me since I recognized the martial spirit of this tribe and knew of what they were capable when commanded by a chief who had gained their

---

[23]"It should be noted that the plan of campaign is drawn up when near the enemy; and supreme authority is vested in the Head Chief."—Milford.

confidence.[24] I already had had occasion to prove it.

My operations were all the more successful since, as I have said above, my military tactics were unknown to the enemy. I also brought the campaign to a speedy close, and to the great glory of the nation. When there were no further enemies to fight, I brought the army back, and the warriors returned to their several homes, for in time of peace the nation does not maintain an army corps. I spent the winter very quietly, visiting different sections of the territory in order to assure myself that everything was tranquil, an activity for which I had the authorization of the district chiefs and council of elders.

The report of the services I had rendered to the nation had spread into all the outlying districts, and everywhere I went I received the most flattering congratulations. The chiefs who assembled every year for the national council, as I said above, decided among themselves to give me renewed testimony of the gratitude that the nation felt it owed me for the services I had rendered it; which is what they did, as one will see.

I AM APPOINTED GRAND WAR CHIEF OR TASTANEGY

On May 5, 1780, all the chiefs of the nation

[24]"I will describe the character and customs of this tribe in Part II."—Milford. See p. 152 ff.

assembled in the town of Tukabahchee[25] to hold
a grand council. When they had discussed affairs
of general interest, one of the band chiefs pointed
out to the assembly that the frequent wars that
the nation was forced to wage, either against the
English or the Anglo-Americans, made it necessary for them to select a Grand Chief having special jurisdiction over all military matters and who
would command the army in the presence of the
enemy.

In view of McGillivray's reputation and the
great confidence that the entire nation had in
his talents, the assembly resolved to offer him
this post. As he was not well and, moreover, was
not much of a warrior, he thanked the assembly
and explained to them that his health was too
poor to sustain the fatigues inseparable from war
and that, if he were forced to accept a post for
which he was so little qualified, the army would
often risk being without a chief, which might
have very unfortunate consequences. At the same
time he explained that if I had merited the respect
and confidence of all the chiefs, either through
my advice or my conduct in former campaigns,
he thought the assembly would not disapprove

[25]The Tukabahchee town, the leading town of the
Upper Creeks, was on the Tallapoosa at the point where
it turns to flow west to meet the Coosa, perhaps thirty
miles east of Little Tallassie. For it see Swanton, *Early
History of the Creek Nation*, 277–282.

of his proposing me for the post of Tastanegy or Grand War Chief.

So all the chiefs, out of respect for McGillivray and affection for me, accepted the proposal. As I was still only Little War Chief, I was not obliged to be present at the deliberations of the assembly; moreover, being utterly ignorant of their designs on my behalf, I was away on some business for the nation when it was decided to appoint me Tastanegy. McGillivray sent a messenger to notify me of this new honor and invite me to come to the assembly to receive this added testimony of their unbounded confidence in me. I returned at once and thanked the assembly with the deepest gratitude for the honor they had just conferred on me, begging them to choose a chief more experienced than I, and explaining that I was not sufficiently acquainted with the national customs to accept a post of such importance; that if I had been so fortunate as to be successful in past wars, I owed this to the wisdom and high efficiency of the band chiefs as well as to the bravery of the warriors; that I preferred to obey rather than to command; and that the nation could count on my most absolute devotion.

After deliberating on my remarks, the assembly decided that I should be invested with the title and authority of Tastanegy or Grand War Chief. [26]

[26]Swanton ("Social Organization of the Creek Con-

Seeing myself thus forced to accept a place of
the highest authority and one that, when dis-
charging the duties of my office, placed me above
the Grand Chief,[27] I informed the assembly that

federacy," 298) says "ordinarily there does not appear to
have been a permanent official of this kind. . . . The position which [Milford] assigns to himself was altogether
superior to that of an ordinary tástánági, but under
McGillivray many innovations were introduced into the
Creek political organization, and a head warrior for the
entire nation may have been one of them." According to
Caleb Swan, who spent months with McGillivray in 1790–
91, the latter in 1782 had "effected a total revolution in
one of their most ancient customs, by placing the warriors
in all cases over the micos or kings, who, though not
active as warriors, were always considered as important
counselors" ("State of the Creek Nation," 281).

[27]Milford wrote *grand chef intérieur*; he meant clearly
the head chief of the nation. "This authority," he added
in a note, "is supreme in time of war, but it only lasts so
long as the war, as I shall explain in Part II" (see pp. 165–
166). Hawkins (*Sketch*, 72) noted that war "is always determined on by the Great Warrior [of the town].
When the Micco and counsellors are of opinion that the
town has been injured, he lifts the war hatchet against the
nation which has injured them. But as soon as it is taken
up, the Micco and counsellors may interpose, and by their
prudent councils [*sic*], stop it, and proceed to adjust the
misunderstanding by negotiation. If the Great Warrior
persists and goes out, he is followed by all who are for
war. It is seldom a town is unanimous, the nation never is;
and within the memory of the oldest man among them, it
is not recollected, that more than one half the nation
have been for war at the same time; or taken, as they express it, the war talk. . . . [Peace] is always determined on
and concluded by the Mic-co and counsellors."

I was ready to do everything they asked of me, that I was deeply appreciative of the honor shown me; but that the gratitude I owed McGillivray, the talents that had made him prominent in the nation before my arrival there, the confidence of which they had given him marked proof in appointing him their Beloved Man, made it incumbent upon me to decline a post that placed me over him; that I could not accept the honorable title offered me unless McGillivray be made Supreme Chief of the nation (at that time he was only Beloved Man); otherwise I should exercise the rights and title of the post in his name. The assembly appreciated my attitude and at once decided to invest McGillivray with the title of Supreme Chief. That way all the political and administrative powers of the nation were vested in his hands, all military powers in mine.[28]

Before the assembly adjourned, it was necessary to institute me as Grand Chief. The ceremonies customary in such instances are numerous and various, and since they are very curious I

[28]Either Milford's memory was uncertain or he seized an opportunity to magnify his importance: the patronage is undoubtedly reversed. If the Frenchman was made head war chief, the reason must lie in McGillivray's power among the Creeks. According to Caughey, during the Revolutionary War the latter was merely one of many chiefs, but by 1783 he had come to sign himself "chief of the Creek Nation" (*McGillivray of the Creeks*, 16, 61).

shall give a detailed description of them in Part II.[29] It will serve to show my influence on the minds of the Indians of North America and how advantageous such influence could be in checking the enterprises of the Anglo-Americans or English.

At the time of my appointment as Grand War Chief, the Indians were allied with the English in their war with the Anglo-Americans. I was informed of the assistance the French were giving the latter, and I could not bring myself to fight for the enemies of my fatherland. I therefore persuaded the savages to maintain neutrality. I pointed out to them that, if peace were concluded between the English and the Anglo-Americans, the latter, in retaliation for the assistance rendered to the English by the Creeks, might well, under some pretext or another, wreak their malice on them, and that they could not be too vigilant in maintaining their troops on a high level so as to be able to repulse any attack directed against them. They appreciated the full force and justice of my arguments, but not wishing to break openly with the English and make an enemy of them, they decided to lend only slight assistance.[30] Al-

[29]See pp. 155–160.

[30]Early in the war McGillivray had been commissioned a colonel by the British and made one of their Indian agents. "He was," says Caughey, "one of the chief factors in securing the British unfaltering support from the Creeks during the war" (*McGillivray of the Creeks*, 16).

though as Grand Chief I was not obliged to take part personally in this war where the nation was merely an auxiliary, nevertheless, fearing lest something should force me to, I decided to undertake a rather long expedition, which I shall here describe in detail.

Since my arrival among the Creeks the old chiefs had often spoken to me of their ancestors and had shown me the strands of beads or sort of chaplet in which their history was recorded. These chaplets represent their public records. They are made of little beads like those we call *perles de Cayenne;* these beads are of divers colors and are strung one right after the other, their signification depending upon the arrangement and the form of bead. As only principal events, without details, are recorded in these strands, it sometimes happens that a single chaplet comprises the history of twenty to twenty-five years. These beads are ranged so as to define exactly the periods of time, and each year can be easily distinguished by those who understand the arrangement. As I was totally ignorant of it and was eager to learn the history of the people that had adopted me and whose interests were as dear to me as those of my own country, I begged the elders to relate it to me orally. The eldest of them, who had the most exact knowledge of the events that befell their forefathers, offered to re-

count to me the history of the Creeks from the
time of their origin: that recorded in the strands
of beads, what his fathers had told him, and what
he himself had witnessed. I gladly accepted an
offer that satisfied so agreeably my curiosity. I
expressed my gratitude to the old man, as well
as my confidence in the history he offered to narrate, and it is this history, as told me by this estimable old man, that I shall relate in Part II of this
work.[31] I will do so all the more confidently since
I myself have been able to verify, on the premises,
most of the things contained in this account. Indeed it was my desire to assure myself in this respect that in part determined me to make the
aforesaid journey, which I am now going to describe.

MY JOURNEY THROUGH THE NATION

Since this journey afforded me the opportunity
of getting to know, in particular, the character of
the Creek nation and the several nations that con-
stitute it, I shall describe it to the reader in great
detail, together with the motives that led me to
undertake it just when I did.

The Indians, as I have said before, had formed
an alliance with the English against the Americans, and since this obliged them to lend the former some assistance, I took advantage of this cir-

[31]See pp. 160–197.

cumstance to travel so as to relieve me of the necessity of taking any part in this war, in which I
knew French interests to be engaged.

To this end I mustered two hundred young
warriors and suggested to them that we go to see
the caverns on the banks, and near the headwaters, of the Red River where their ancestors
had lived. They replied that if I wished to conduct them there they were ready to go with me.
I therefore made all the necessary preparations
for our journey, and we set out on February 1,
1781, departing from Little Tallassie (where I resided with McGillivray) half a league beyond old
Fort Toulouse.[32]

I directed my course northward to the territory of the Upper Choctaws, with whose chief
(called Mastabe[33] as I am called Tastanegy) I was
acquainted, in order to prevent his sending warriors to aid the English who, I knew, had won the
adherence of the Lower Choctaws. I told him that
the French had espoused the cause of the Anglo-
Americans and that, if he went into the war, it

[32]Fort Toulouse had been built by the French in 1714
and abandoned at the close of the French and Indian
War.

[33]According to Dr. John R. Swanton *mastabe* is a Choctaw word meaning "(to) go (to war) and kill." Milford
would have traveled west, not north, to the Choctaw
country. This man was probably Franchimastabe, leading
chief of the Choctaws at this time (Kinnaird, *Spain in the
Mississippi Valley*, passim).

should be on the side of the latter. He followed my advice.

Leaving the Choctaws I proceeded to Mobile where on arrival I kept with me only five Indians, ordering the others to go on to the farthest end of Lake Pontchartrain, cross the Mississippi, and wait for me on the other side opposite Iberville River.

I stopped several days in Mobile. In that city there is a fort built of bricks.[34] At that time the fort and town were commanded by a French creole named Favrot[35] in the service of the King of Spain. I called on him, and, when he learned that I was French, he overwhelmed me with courtesies and made me promise to come to see him again during my stay. I gave him my word and I kept it with very great pleasure.

One day when we were out walking and went to visit the fort, we had occasion to cross a sort of bridge made of a single plank about fifteen feet by three, which was thrown over a ravine. After passing to the other side, he drew my attention to it and said that the French Government had

[34]Fort Condé, according to Bartram (*Travels*, 402). For a description see Hamilton, *Colonial Mobile*, 137–138.

[35]Pierre Favrot commanded at Mobile from 28 June 1784 to 28 June 1887. In 1781 when Milford declared he met him at Mobile, he was in command at Baton Rouge (*Favrot Papers*, Vol. III). There is no mention of Milford in the *Favrot Papers*.

paid for it. He asked me how much I thought it had cost, and noting my hesitancy in replying to his question, he said: "That bridge cost France thirty thousand francs, and since I've been commandant here I've renewed it twice without its costing the King of Spain a penny. The fort we're going to visit cost France enormous sums, and it is utterly worthless—a four-pounder could demolish it in two hours."

The town of Mobile is pleasantly situated on a river of the same name; the water, however, is brackish and disagreeable to drink so that the inhabitants and the garrison have to fetch what they need from a stream about a league from town, of which the water is excellent.[36] This is a

[36]"The city of Mobile is situated on the easy ascent of a rising bank, extending near half a mile back on the level plain above; it has been near a mile in length, though now [1777] chiefly in ruins, many houses vacant and mouldering to earth; yet there are a few good buildings inhabited by French gentlemen, English, Scotch and Irish, and emigrants from the Northern British colonies. . . . The principal French buildings are constructed of brick, and are of one story, but on an extensive scale, four square, encompassing on three sides a large area or court yard: the principal apartment is on the side fronting the street; they seem in some degree to have copied after the Creek habitation in the general plan: those of the poorer class are constructed of a strong frame of Cypress, filled in with brick, plaistered and white-washed inside and out" (Bartram, *Travels*, 402). Hutchins a few years later reported Mobile "a very considerable place. It has a small regular fort, built with brick, and a neat square of barracks for the

great inconvenience but would be easy to remedy by means of a canal turning the course of the rivulet so as to pass by the fort—an operation that would cost very little. The town has scarcely more than forty property owners, and each has a plantation up the river, which they call their *desert*.[37]

Today, in virtue of the agreement between Spain and the Anglo-Americans, all the plantations belonging to the inhabitants of Mobile are under the jurisdiction of the Americans.[38] On this land there is a large quantity of live oaks, cedars and other timber suitable for building ships, which would be of the greatest advantage to France for its navy.

The people of Mobile do an extensive business with pitch. In winter they have their negroes gather resinous trees or pitch pines. They then stack them in piles more or less like those for making charcoal erected by the charcoal burners in European forests. When the stack is fairly

officers and soldiers" (*Topographical Description of Louisiana, and West-Florida*, 69–70).

[37]Cleared lands or cultivated fields were so-called in local French usage (see McDermott, *A Glossary of Mississippi Valley French*, 66).

[38]Milford probably referred to the Pinckney Treaty of 1795 and the line run by Andrew Ellicott, 1798–99. Galvez had taken the town from the British in March, 1780, and it remained in Spanish hands until its capture by American troops in April, 1813.

high, they dig round it a little trench, which slopes gradually down into a basin proportionate in size to the pile of timber. As soon as they set fire to this wood, a large quantity of pitch flows out of it, which the negroes collect and put into vats. I have seen such stacks of wood produce up to two hundred vats of pitch, which in the spring is sold very cheaply in Mobile. Before employing the pine in this way to get pitch, these settlers first extract the turpentine. This is how they do it. They make a sloping incision in the tree about one foot from the ground and place a receptacle underneath it to catch the sap that exudes through this tap; every morning they then come to collect what has run into the receptacle and put it in casks. This juice is turpentine. It is only gathered when the sap is running because this operation usually kills the tree, which in dying becomes astoundingly enriched with oleo-resin and forms the fat pitch pines that later serve to produce the pitch.[39]

Mobile is a little earthly paradise, which is why I often went there. The inhabitants, while not rich, are perfectly happy there. Hunting and fishing are very plentiful, and the fruits and vegetables are as excellent as in Europe. The people

[39]Bernard Romans (*History of East and West Florida*, 149–153) and Bartram (*Travels*, 416–417) also describe the making of turpentine and pitch.

of Mobile are very good hunters; they are very adroit at shooting birds on the fly; they always keep one or more loaded rifles behind the door of the house, and, since large quantities of water fowl such as wild ducks, terns, and others pass frequently over the city, the inhabitants on sighting them take their rifles and shoot at them. In this way they kill a fairly large quantity for their own use without being obliged to go hunting at a distance.

Upon leaving Mobile I went to Pascagoula. The inhabitants of this village are very lazy; but since they have little ambition, they are happy and lead a perfectly tranquil existence. For the most part they are Bohemians married with Indian women. There are some French creoles amongst them. They are all carpenters and build the schooners for the coasting-trade in Mobile Bay, New Orleans, and Pensacola.[40]

I next mounted Pearl River to the extremity of Bay St. Louis where I found very beautiful plantations belonging to French creoles whose ancestors came from Bordeaux.[41] They are very happy and seem to have no desire to go back to Europe. They are hospitable, kind to strangers,

[40]According to Le Page du Pratz the settlers of Pascagoulas were Canadians (*Histoire de la Louisiane*, II, 214, 255).

[41]Pearl River does not empty in Bay St. Louis but into Lake Borgne about twenty-five miles to the west.

treat them regally, and are sorry to see them leave. I stayed several days with these creoles, and they received me in the most friendly way. I left them to go to New Orleans via Lake Pontchartrain and Bayou St. Jean at the entrance of which there is a wooden fort built by the French, which is very well preserved and is still good for some time yet.[42] It is at present equipped with the same guns left there by the French, but they are made of bad iron and are good for nothing, and I think it would be dangerous to use them. From the fort to the town of New Orleans is about two leagues.

The governor of this town is named Miró and the intendant Navarro.[43] I am going to give an idea of the manner in which these two men administer the finances of the King of Spain in this region.

ADMINISTRATION OF THE SPANISH GOVERNORS

Every year the Spanish government sends five hundred thousand piastres to New Orleans for

[42] "The entrance to the Bayouk of St. John is defended by a battery of five or six guns" (Hutchins, *Topographical Description of Louisiana, and West-Florida*, 36–37).

[43] It is impossible to say in what year Milford first visited New Orleans but certainly not in 1781. Estevan Miró had been second in command there to Galvez since 1779 and was acting governor from 1781. He did not actually become governor until Galvez' promotion in 1785. Martin Navarro was intendant from 1780 to 1788.

the expenses of the colony. These piastres arrive from Havana every six months at the rate of two hundred and fifty thousand at a time. Between the arrival of the galleons money is fairly scarce. In order to supply it the governor and the intendant obtained from the King of Spain permission to issue paper money. When this paper money goes into circulation, the silver disappears, and in consequence there is always a considerable loss. I have seen this paper currency at a loss of seventy-five and eighty livres per hundred, and I can certify to the fact that in 1783 the loss was as much as eighty-five livres per hundred. When the paper money dropped to this point, the governor and intendant bought it up, and immediately upon the arrival of the galleon (of which they received advance notice since the ships did not always arrive at a stated time) it went back to par, or only slightly below. They then restored it to circulation and in this way gained enormous sums. The inhabitants, seeing themselves thus despoiled of the fruit of their labor, neglected commerce and the cultivation of the land, both of which were almost utterly destroyed by this juggling with the public funds. Complaints were addressed to the Spanish Court, and the King, on being informed of the matter, recalled the intendant and the governor and sent in their place Baron de Carondelet, who had the title of Captain-general, protector, and intendant of Louisiana and the two Floridas.[44]

I will not close this article without speaking of the administration of this virtuous man of whose frankness and loyalty I have often had personal proof.[45]

ADMINISTRATION OF BARON DE CARONDELET

This new governor had no sooner arrived than he perceived the pernicious effect of the paper money, which paralyzed everything. He abolished it and by this retirement forced silver back into circulation. Commerce was immediately revitalized, the inhabitants laid out plantations and engaged in every possible kind of speculation. They

[44]Milford's report is somewhat confused. Navarro resigned 25 February 1788; Miró was named intendant in his place and held both offices until the close of 1791, when he was succeeded by Carondelet. Paper money had been issued at New Orleans as early as 1780 (the silver came from Vera Cruz rather than Havana); its withdrawal from circulation (on Miró's recommendation) was authorized by Spain in 1788. Depreciation of the paper did reach seventy per cent in 1785 and a higher percentage later. There seems to have been no ground for charges against Miró and Navarro. For detailed consideration of this matter of finance see Burson, *The Stewardship of Don Estaban Miró*, 86–100, 285–299.

[45]The virtuous Carondelet hardly returned the Frenchman's good opinion: he wrote to McGillivray 14 September 1792 "My intention never was to employ Milfort except in expeditions which require more handwork than headwork" (Caughey, *McGillivray of the Creeks*, 338).

led a tranquil, happy existence under the wise and kindly administration of Baron de Carondelet until 1793, when war broke out between France and Spain. At that time the French creoles, learning of the revolution that had taken place in France and ignorant alike of its goal and its result, tried to foment trouble in the colony and thereby forced the governor to take vigorous measures against those whom he could not recall to order by mildness and persuasion.[46] Many of them left the colony and went to the United States.

Before leaving New Orleans, the capital of Louisiana, I am going to give the reader an idea of the importance of this region and of the advantages that France could derive from its possession. In order to enable the government to appreciate fully this advantage, I shall go into details that could only be given by a man thoroughly acquainted with the country, that is, not only with Louisiana but with all the contiguous colonies, and I can assure the government that there is no one in France who could give it more exact particulars, and that it should distrust those persons who claim to be well informed in this respect and who, in order to cloak their false in-

[46]Carondelet took office in New Orleans 30 December 1791. On 15 February 1793 he reported to Las Casas, Captain General of Cuba, evidences of French revolutionary activities in New Orleans and issued a proclamation forbidding dissemination of revolutionary propaganda.

formation, have taken pains to calumniate me as an adventurer seeking to impose myself on the First Consul and abuse his good faith. I ask nothing of my detractors but to imitate my frankness and to come out into the open as I am doing. If their advice is good they need not fear my censure; if it is bad it is my duty to notify the government; then it is up to the latter, in its wisdom, to decide what should be done. With this I resume my narrative.

To give the government of France an idea of the importance the Americans attach to gaining the affection and adherence of the Indians of North America—and they know how much this means—I shall quote herewith an article that appeared in the *Gazette de France,* 4 Floreal, Year 10 [April 24, 1802], which says:

The government of the United States seems to have already succeeded, up to a certain point, in its enterprise of civilizing the Indian tribes known as the Creeks, which are dispersed over the territory situated south of the Ohio. It has prevailed upon the natives of these districts to appoint six deputies from each tribe, who will meet in May every year to hold a national council to which the delegates of each tribe will submit a report of the state of the nation and consider ways and means of ameliorating it. They will likewise discuss any possible subjects of grievance on the part of the Indians regarding any offences committed in violation of their treaty stipulations with the United States that they believe give them ground for complaint. The council will appoint a speaker and, from the opening of the council till its closure, the sittings will be permanent so that there will be no interruption of the discussions either by day or by night. The Indian deputies will eat and sleep in the building where the sittings are held and they will be furnished, at the expense of the American Government, with beef, corn, beans, and salt. It has already been estimated that the cost of maintenance for the duration of these annual sessions will not exceed the sum of 400 dollars.

The raising of livestock seems to be part of the plan of civilization envisaged for the Creeks, and no obstacle whatsoever stands in the way of its realization. Since their land offers, at all seasons of the year, abundant food and excellent pasturage for horses as well as sheep and horned cattle, they will experience no difficulty in cultivating this branch of rural economy; and the Indians, lazy by nature, take quickly to any ideas that are easy to carry out.

The inhabitants of several large towns, who had exhausted the lands in their neighborhood by culture, were very loath to leave and settle out in scattered villages situated in a more fertile region; and at the beginning of last spring seventy ploughs were procured and issued to them. Five thousand young peach trees were also obtained for them, and they have made haste to plant them.

At first there was strong opposition on the part of the tribal chiefs to the introduction of manufactures; they feared that, if their women could clothe and feed themselves by their own exertions, they might dream of becoming independent of the men and of shaking off the degrading yoke under which the latter please to hold them. But these fears have been dissipated all the more readily in that experience has convinced them that the family link is more firm and the affections fortified in proportion as the women are more useful and more assiduously occupied in domestic concerns. After spinning for two years, several Indian women have been able to clothe themselves with the product of their labor and have even acquired some hogs and cattle. These examples have proved such a stimulus to their countrywomen that last spring they applied to the agents of English factories for one hundred pairs of cotton cards and eighty spinning wheels, which were at once delivered to them. One has already seen—and not without surprise—the head of an Indian family make a loom and two spinning wheels by hand.

In order to prevent any crimes or abuses, in the autumn every hunting party in going out must report to the chief of the tribe who will charge one of them to keep watch over the conduct of the others and who will be answerable for the conduct of his companions. When the hunters return, each chief will make a report in person to the agent of the American Government stating what they have done or what they have seen during their expedition.

Two blacksmith shops have already been opened in Creek territory at the expense of the United States, and, though all this does not represent any great advance in civilization, it is always a step forward in the right direction. The arts in Europe no doubt only arrived at their present degree of perfection in this way.

The agent appointed by the government of the United States to attend the national council of the Creeks will fulfill there the functions of Minister of Justice. In this, one can only applaud the wise policy that seems to have dictated this measure. The time is perhaps not far off when the United States will represent a colossal power, which will concentrate in its hands all the armed force, all the commerce, and all the glory of the New World.

If I did not know the Creek nation through and through, I confess that, after the above-quoted article, I would regard it as completely under the heel of the Americans; but I know too well the Indians' love of independence and their hatred of the Anglo-Americans not to appreciate this article at its just value. In order to enable the reader to judge the truth of its contents, I shall analyze it for him, along with the motives that inspired it.

The Anglo-Americans announce that they have begun to civilize the Indians located south of the Ohio. The only refutation that I shall make of this statement is that there are no savages south of this river—all the tribes are in the east and the west.[47]

As regards the six deputies per tribe who are to hold a national assembly in May of each year, it will be recalled that I have already written that this is the time of their general assembly.[48] The

[47]So Milford wrote. Can it be that his knowledge of geography was faulty?

[48]Milford was right in insisting that the national assembly was an old Creek institution: Bossu reported it in

author of the article has also religiously held
to their custom of not leaving the assembly
either by day or by night till all business is concluded.

The Americans say that the Creeks have consented to raise their cattle because the land inhabited by these Indians abounds in excellent
pasturage. One can easily judge the truth of this
assertion on learning that no tribe owns such
quantities of livestock of every description as the
Creeks. It does not seem likely that they would
be willing to relinquish their own cattle just for
the privilege of raising that of the Americans.[49]

They state that they have given the Creeks
ploughs and looms. This is possible; but with
respect to the five thousand peach trees they
claim to have distributed, the author has no

1759. For a full summary of its history and workings see
Swanton, "Social Organization of the Creek Confederacy," 310–327. The author of the account in the *Gazette
de France*, however, was probably referring to an attempt
by the Indian Agent Benjamin Hawkins to make the government more stable. Perhaps Hawkins overstated the
case when he claimed "the Creeks never had, till this year
[1799], a national government and law. . . . The attempt,
in the course of the last and present year, to establish a
national council, to meet annually, and to make general
regulations for the welfare of the nation, promises to succeed" (*Sketch*, 67).

[49]Milford seems to misinterpret here: the quoted text
clearly means the raising of cattle by the Creeks for themselves as a way of business.

doubt forgotten, or never known, that the Creeks have such an enormous quantity of peach trees that one encounters them at every turn. After this, one may judge the importance of this gift.

In order to prevent crimes and abuses during the hunt, they have required each band of hunters to present themselves to the chief of their tribe, who will charge one of them to keep an eye on the others and who will be answerable for the conduct of his companions. I know so well how the Creeks would rebel at such a suggestion that I guarantee that if an American, were he the President himself, should attempt to make such a suggestion in the assembly of the chiefs of the nation he would never leave it alive.

The task of keeping order during the hunt rests with the head of each family who is responsible for what happens in his own; and the Grand Chief of the nation himself does not have the right to intermeddle in this control, which besides is not difficult, seeing that no crime is ever committed there.

Consequently nothing, or practically nothing, in this article is true; and it was only written to try to persuade the French Government that the Government of the United States has already made great progress towards gaining the confidence of these tribes, something indeed that it has long coveted and that it would be dangerous to let it gain, but of which it is a simple matter to deprive it.

With respect to the authority over the Creek nation, which the article already attributes to the Anglo-Americans, if it were such as it states, I should not advise the French to risk taking possession of Louisiana, for they would not hold it long; the perfidious innuendoes of the Americans would soon evoke against them those river massacres where every single Frenchman was slaughtered by the Natchez.[50]

However much the Americans may boast—and they think they are already cock of the walk—I know that it is still easy to set bounds to their ambition and that France is perhaps the only power capable of undertaking it and of carrying it through successfully, the result depending very largely on the wisdom and knowledge of the men that it employs. The establishment of the French in this part of the continent would be of inestimable advantage, for it would save from bondage to the Americans all the tribes scattered over the immense spaces of the continent, and prevent any encroachment on the peace of Europe, which they already have the impudence to menace with their future authority.

[50]Milford refers apparently to the destruction of the Natchez Post and the massacre of the French in 1729.

To make known to the French Government, in particular, how greatly it is to its interest to establish itself firmly in this part of the continent, I am going to describe some of the localities and prove to it that whatever power gets control of Louisiana and the beautiful Mississippi River will be able very easily to dictate the laws to all those having possessions on this continent. I shall begin with the Mississippi River.

DESCRIPTION OF THE MISSISSIPPI

The Mississippi is a very large river situated in lower Louisiana. It has made a bed in the form of a bayou, seventy leagues in length, in which it carries its waters to the sea. This bed has been formed by the large quantity of trees annually brought down the river when the snow and ice melts at the source. It is impossible to check this timber, which every year forms new islands, stemming the waters of the sea and driving them back farther from New Orleans. The raft usually brings with it such a large quantity of mud and sand that it quickly forms habitable ground. There are already many such places with beautiful plantations, but they are small in extent because the sea is on one side of the river and Lake Pontchartrain on the other, the result being that in this section Louisiana is so closely pressed that the breadth of the cultivable soil does not exceed half a league. The rest is unworkable and shifting.

I have noted trees of enormous size along the banks of this river, but they are of poor quality and cannot be used for construction because the worms attack them as soon as they are felled and a ship constructed of this timber would not last six years. Nevertheless there is a very great quantity of good timber in the country, but it is in another section.

In its widest part the Mississippi is about one third of a league in breadth, with a depth of eighty fathoms; but the entire bed is covered with trees, which are so intertwined that, if a ship, wishing to cast anchor, lets go the anchor, it cannot haul it in again and has to cut the cable. It has no other recourse than to make fast to the trees along the river bank.

Fifty years ago the river was no broader than the Seine, but the current is so rapid that it has worn away the banks and has made a very broad river bed. I have sometimes seen ground from twenty to thirty toises[51] in width and more than a league in length give way and be engulfed in an instant. This happens when the river is low after the snow thaws, and it is this that makes it so dangerous for ships going upstream; they can-

[51]The *toise* was six French or 6.3945 English feet; the French league equalled 2.2449 English miles.

not avoid skirting the shore, and when the wind is not favorable they must be towed and even bushwacked.[52] There was a *balise* where pilots stayed, but it has been several times destroyed by the river and re-formed, and now there is nothing left but a wretched house occupied by a few pilots. The little block house was completely demolished, and the Spanish have now built another fifteen leagues farther up the river, which they call Fort Plaquemine. It is the only one defending the approach to New Orleans from the river.[53]

The passes are variable, and it is now very difficult to enter this river from the sea. This would be so hard to remedy that I regard it as impossible in view of the changes in the course of the river. Sometimes one pass is free, sometimes

[52]"Ils sont forcés de touer et même de s'amarrer aux arbres sur les bords," Milford wrote. To bushwhack is to propel a boat by pulling on bushes or trees along the shore.

[53]Hutchins noted that the original Balize post, built by the French in 1734, had been replaced by Ulloa in 1766 with another near the southeast entrance to the river (*Topographical Description of Louisiana, and West-Florida,* 33–34). Carondelet in the early 1790's built there a new blockhouse defended by two cannons and housing twenty-four men. This is not to be confused with Fort Plaquemine (ten cannons) below the English Turn. A detailed report on the defenses of New Orleans by Carondelet, 24 November 1794, will be found in Robertson, *Louisiana under Spain, France, and the United States,* II, 310–332.

another, so that any work to regulate the course could be undone in an instant. The pass formerly known as Grand Pass is now scarcely navigable because of the tremendous number of little islets formed by this river, and the earth and the sand that it brings with it, leaving a depth of only about twelve feet. Of the five former passes, only two now remain, the southern and the southwestern. They have a depth of about fourteen feet at the bar. Here one finds a hard sand, banked up by the current of the river and the reflux of the tide, which represents a menace for any vessel happening to go aground on it. If a vessel is caught in a calm, it risks being carried by the current into St. Bernard Bay, from which it is very difficult to get out.[54] It requires great experience in navigating these waters to avoid this sand bank.

If France should permit the Anglo-Americans to become masters of this beautiful river, in fifty years' time they would be dictating the laws to Europe. All the West Indies, which they regard as part of their continent, would be under their domination, as well as Mexico and Peru, which

---

[54]Vermilion Bay was so-called in the late eighteenth century, according to Hutchins, who located a village of "Tuckapas" six leagues west of New Iberia "on the Vermilion river, which runs into the bay of St. Bernard" (*Topographical Description of Louisiana, and West-Florida.* 47).

they could very easily take away from the Spanish. It was no doubt to further the execution of this project that they wished to insinuate to the French Government that the part of Louisiana situated on the left bank of the Mississippi is a tongue of marshy land composed of shifting sands, the possession of which is of slight importance to France but presents certain advantages to the United States from the military point of view.

The list given below of the commodities brought down the Mississippi from Cumberland and Kentucky shows the richness of these two new provinces, which the Americans took from the Indians. It also shows the importance of free traffic on the river.[55]

---

[55] "Extract from the [*National*] *Intelligencer*, an American newspaper published at Washington, 4 November 1801.

"Statement of the commodities exported down the Mississippi agreeably to the Customs House Books from 1st January 1801 to 30th June following in four hundred and forty flat boats, twenty-six keel boats and seven large canoes.

"62,033 barrels flour
882 hhds. tobacco
43 packs peltry (a)
1,990 same ditto (b)
557 bear skins (c)
5,347 deer skins
25,000 same ditto (d)
30 bales hemp
22,746 same ditto (e)

57,692 wt. ham (f)
680 barrels pork
43 beef
129,600 wt. tar'd cordage (g)
77,042 wt. white rope (h)
565 barrels whisky
29 ditto peach brandy
30 ditto cider
71 ditto butter (i)

I have exposed the perfidy of the American in-
sinuation by recalling to the Government of
France that it is upon this negligible land that
New Orleans is built and a large number of excellent plantations up as far as Iberville River,
from there to Baton Rouge, where there is a fort
defending the river, and finally up to the con-
fines of the United States formed by Bayou
Chaudpisse, representing one hundred and twenty leagues and including the most fertile land in
the colony. I described in detail this *little piece of
land* in the *Gazette de France* of Thursday, 10
Thermidor, year 10 [July 29, 1802], and I have
proved to the government that the arrangement

1,770 wt. bar iron	2,240 barrels apples
112 barrels powder (j)	22 boxes window glass
94 barrels beer (k)	30 barrels onions
14 same (l)	16 boxes soap
4,154 bales cotton (average 300	10 millstones
pounds each)	3 schooners and 1 brig
	built on the Ohio"
	—Milford.

Milford's figures are slightly in error. Corrections from
the *Intelligencer* are as follows:

    (a)　45
    (b)　1980
    (c)　657
    (d)　next item was omitted: 56,900 wt. lead in pigs
    (e)　*Sic.* More likely lead than hemp.
    (f)　Bacon
    (g)　29,600
    (h)　67,000
    (i)　beer
    (j)　Listed as nails, not powder
    (k)　Listed as 94 barrels pigs lard
    (l)　Listed as 14 firkens butter

suggested by the President of the United States aims at nothing less than making the Anglo-Americans masters of all the ports and anchorages where French vessels might enter, so that one could not even go up the Mississippi river without the permission of the United States.

The treaty that Spain concluded with them three years ago, by which it ceded the town and fort of Natchez, as well as all the villages, forts, and other military posts that it received from the French up as far as the Illinois, and of which a part of the inhabitants are French creoles, has already given them an immense advantage. I have no doubt that the Prince of Peace, who concluded the treaty in 1798, was taken in, and now France must bear the brunt of it since, instead of recovering everything that she ceded to Spain, she finds herself deprived of the most beautiful territory in the world and one that would have offered her the most valuable resources.[56] I know this country in and out, having travelled all over

[56]By the Treaty of San Lorenzo, concluded by Thomas Pinckney and Manuel Godoy (later Principe de la Paz), Spain in 1795 accepted the 31st parallel as the northern boundary of the Floridas and conceded navigation of the Mississippi; but the Memphis, Vicksburg, Natchez areas were not surrendered until 1798. The posts above the Ohio had, of course, passed thirty years earlier from the French to the British.

it in the course of twenty years; I know how advantageous it could be and I have already described it to the Government, which relieves me
of the necessity of now going into greater detail.
I shall therefore limit myself here to the remark
that, if things remain as they are, it might have
unfortunate consequences for Spain.[57]

CONTINUATION OF MY JOURNEY AMONG
THE TRIBES OF THE CREEK NATION

I therefore left New Orleans and its paper
money to rejoin my band on the right bank of the
Mississippi opposite Iberville River, where I had
fixed the rendezvous. I next continued my course
in a southerly direction and before long arrived
at St. Bernard Bay, situated 29° 5″ north latitude, meridian of Paris. In this bay there is a
beautiful river, which flows from east to west for
about thirty leagues and then veers to south-
southwest.[58] I believe the source is in Mexico,
and it was probably by following its course that
the Atakapas came to settle at the farther end of

[57] "I shall give the reasons in a more extended work."—
Milford. This "extended" work remains hidden in obscu-
rity. Milford's efforts to win attention in France are discussed in the editor's introduction.

[58] It is impossible to identify this river. From a point
near Plaquemine on the Mississippi (below Baton Rouge)
he moved south to Vermilion Bay and then westerly to the
Atakapa country in the southwestern part of Louisiana.
See note 54, p. 56.

St. Bernard Bay when they were compelled to flee from Mexico, their native country.

We left St. Bernard Bay without having seen any savages and took a westerly course. The fifth day of march, an hour after sunrise, my scouts returned to report that a quarter of a league ahead of us, in a little field on the edge of a pond, there was a group of Indians, men and women, who they thought were smoking meat.

ARRIVAL AMONG THE ATAKAPAS

We were then in quite a dense forest so that none of my band had been seen. I formed them into three detachments and disposed them so as to encompass these Indians, leaving no avenue of escape but the side towards the pond. I then ordered my men to advance and sent a little chief to ascertain to what tribe these savages belonged and what their intentions might be with respect to us. We soon learned that they were Atakapas, who the moment they saw us, far from showing any hostility, made signs of peace and amity to us. There were one hundred and eighty of them, of both sexes, busy—as we surmised—in smoking meat. As soon as my three detachments emerged from the forest, one of these savages came directly up to me; I saw at once that he was not an Atakapa. He addressed me politely and with an ease of manner unusual among these savages. He offered me refreshments for my band, which I accepted with thanks. They served food to the entire detachment, and during the six hours or so that I spent with this man I learned that he was an European, that he had been a Jesuit, and that when he went to Mexico these people had chosen him to be their chief. He spoke French fairly well. He told me that his name was Joseph, but I did not learn what part of Europe he came from.

He said that the name *Atakapa,* meaning man-eater, was given to that nation by the Spanish because whenever they caught a Spaniard they roasted him, but they did not eat him;[59] that they did so in order to avenge the tortures inflicted on their ancestors by the Spanish when they came to take possession of Mexico; that if any English or French were lost in this bay the Atakapas treated them kindly and offered them hospitality; and if the former did not desire to remain with them, they took them to the Arkansas whence they could easily reach New Orleans.

He said to me: "Here you have approximately half the Atakapa nation; the other half is on ahead. We are in the habit of separating into two or three bands when we hunt bison which, in the spring, go back to the west and, in the au-

[59]Hodge (*Handbook of North American Indians,* I, 114) derives the name from Choctaw words meaning "eats man."

tumn, descend to these latitudes. Herds of them sometimes go as far as the Missouri. We kill them with arrows, our young hunters being very skilful in this hunt. Besides, these animals are very numerous and are as tame as though they were reared on a farm. We also take great care never to frighten them. When they are on a prairie or in a forest, we camp near them so as to accustom them to seeing us, and we follow all their movements so that they can never get away. Their flesh serves us for food and their hides for clothing. I've now been with this tribe about eleven years; I'm happy and contented and haven't the slightest desire to return to Europe. I have six children whom I love very dearly and with whom I wish to end my days."

When my band was rested and refreshed, I took leave of Joseph and the Atakapas, assuring them of my desire to repay their hospitality, and I resumed my journey.

The interior of this immense tract of country on the right bank of the Mississippi abounds with bison or wild cattle and Andalusian horses, which have escaped from Mexico where they were brought by the Spanish.[60] Those found on the banks of the Missouri are of another breed and of an extraordinary height and size. The smallest

[60]The latest and fullest accounts of the wild horses are Dobie's *The Mustangs* and Roe's *The Indian and his Horse.*

are as big as our largest European horses. The way the Indians catch them is very adroit. They throw them by firing at the horse's neck; at a distance of one hundred paces they are sure of cutting off the mane and of just grazing the neck. Stunned by the shot, the horse falls, and the Indians immediately rush up, shackle it, and lead it away; they tame it then easily. To this end, the Indians walk the horse through a marsh till it is tired out, or else they exhaust it in the same way in a river. When the horse is thus subdued, it becomes very gentle. There are very few that are untamable.

ARRIVAL AMONG THE NATCHITOCHES
AND THE ARKANSAS

I held continually to a west-northwesterly course, and after traversing immense forests and vast prairies with numerous ponds, I arrived among the Natchitoches, who live a little southwest of the Red River, near the Mississippi.[61] They are a rather small tribe, very docile and hospitable, and very fond of the French. They own the best land in Louisiana. It is so fertile that it brings forth without any cultivation all the seeds one wants to sow.

[61]The Natchitoches lived near the post of that name on the Red River at least one hundred miles (crow-flight) from the Mississippi.

From there we came to the White River, where we fell in with a small band of Arkansas [Quapaws] and some French creoles.[62] We then returned to the Red River and, as this was the goal of our journey, the sole motive of which was to satisfy the curiosity of the young Creek warriors who had asked me to conduct them to the headwaters of this river so that they might visit the caves inhabited by their forefathers after their flight from Mexico, we decided to mount the river, holding close to its banks.

ARRIVAL AT RED RIVER

The Red River empties its water into the Mississippi at 32° N and 90° W, meridian of Paris. It rises in Mexican territory at 36° N, so that it flows from south to north.[63] In going upstream I fell in with a part of the Choctaw nation, which twenty-five years before had set out to find land where game was plentiful. These Choctaws are sometimes at war with the Caddos, a belligerent and wicked nation with which it is dangerous to have any traffic on account of its doubledeal-

[62]What stream Milford could mean by the White River it is impossible to say. Does he possibly intend to say that they ventured as far north as the White River of Arkansas and then turned back to the Red?

[63]*Sic!* Red River, of course, rises in the panhandle of Texas (then Mexican) about 35° north and enters the Mississippi about 31°.

ing.[64] They often sell their peltry to foreign traders and then kill the traders to recover it again. They are the best dressers of bison and beaver skins, which they hunt in large quantities.

When we had ascended the Red River to a point about one hundred and fifty leagues beyond its conflux with the Mississippi, we passed through a beautiful forest and, on coming out of it, espied the caverns of which the elders had often spoken.[65] I instantly recognized them from the description. The caves were located on the banks of the Red River on an eminence that the English call a "Bloff." Those I examined were capable of housing fifteen to twenty thousand families. They are situated quite close together. I fired my gun several times whilst going through them, and a great number of bison, wild cattle, and even horses rushed out of them. We caught at least five hundred of the latter. I noted from the terror of the bison that, when this animal is fear-stricken, even the highest precipices do not stop them. I have seen more than four thousand of them plunge headlong from the caves into the Red River despite the height of over eighty feet. The wild bull is not so reckless; he avoids a

[64]For the Caddos consult Swanton, *History and Ethnology of the Caddo Indians.*

[65]This would have carried Milford to a point fifty or one hundred miles beyond the present east boundary of Oklahoma.

precipice if he feels that he is not strong or nimble enough to take the leap. These wild cattle come from Mexico. They scatter through the forests and over the prairies and multiply so rapidly that it is not at all unusual to run across more than ten thousand of them in a day's march.

ARRIVAL AT THE CAVES

We arrived at the caves near Christmas, 1781, that is, at the beginning of winter. As the region is rather cold and we had to cross a good many rivers and the trails were now very bad, I proposed to my warriors that we stop in the caves to await the spring; they agreed to this. We picked out the most commodious and stayed there seventy-five days, during which time we had food in abundance and lived very comfortably. My warriors spent their time hunting, fishing, and dancing.

DEPARTURE FROM THE CAVES AND RETURN TO THE NATION

When spring came, we prepared to set off again and return to the nation. I noticed that my young warriors were loath to leave this beautiful solitude where their forefathers had dwelt so long and that brought back to them such tender memories of the past.

We left at the end of March, 1782, taking a

south-southwest by westerly course.[66] We journeyed for more than two hundred leagues in this direction without encountering a single forest—nothing but prairies and land that appeared to me to be very fertile and was teeming with all sorts of wild animals which, wanting for nothing, lived in peace. We found neither streams nor rivers, only ponds and little lakes, the water of which was, for the most part, brackish. We usually camped, in so far as possible, on the shores of those with fresh water. Here we found a large quantity of dried rushes, which we used for cooking our meat. When this resource was lacking, we had to fall back on dried droppings.[67] Nevertheless, we found in this immense stretch of territory a rather fine spring that I believe is the source of the White River, which empties its waters into the Mississippi at 34° 40″ N and 90° 32″ W, meridian of Paris. The Little Pani nation lives on this river, and at its mouth, to the east, are the Arkansas [Quapaws], a portion of which we encountered on the White River.[68] We crossed over

[66]Could the "sud-sud-ouest quart d'ouest" of the text be a misprint for "north-northwest"? Five hundred miles southwest would carry them to, say, the Pecos and the Rio Grande—northwest, to the Arkansas in western Kansas. Only by such correction can any sense possibly be made of these wanderings.

[67]Buffalo chips.

[68]By "petite nation des Panis" Milford probably meant the Panis Noirs or Panis Piqués (Wichitas) on the Red

without stopping and, after several days march, came to the banks of the Missouri River, which I was looking for. We followed its course across vast plains similar to those we had just traversed. From time to time we traveled through quite fine forests in which we found no trace of man. After passing through a number we came to one that I imagined was the one in which the Creeks had surprised and defeated the Alibamus, since along the banks of the river we noted some rather beautiful caverns.[69]

We crossed over to the left bank of the Missouri on the west side of the river and had not gone far when we ran into and surprised fifteen Indians who were lying asleep on the edge of a pond. They were very amazed to see us and received us with open arms, giving us to understand that they lived in a forest about three leagues distant, which they pointed out to us. They had some bison and deer skins with them and a considerable quantity of beaver skins. I had them make them into bundles, which they loaded on their shoulders; and as they had muskets, I ordered my young warriors to take them up, and I then made these savages

River. By White River he here obviously intends the affluent of the Arkansas. If there is truth in this travel report, he must have reached the Arkansas River, not the White which rises in the Ozarks.

[69]See the history of the tribe reported by Milford, pp. 178–179.

march between two platoons. I detached one of them and, giving him back his musket, powder horn, and balls, motioned to him to go on to his settlement and notify them of our coming. He started off at once with great alacrity, turning round, however, from time to time to see if we were following him with his fourteen companions. We soon lost sight of him and, when we were about half a league from the forest where these Indians—who are called Osages—lived, we saw about a hundred of both sexes come out to meet us.[70] They received us with very evident pleasure and immediately on our arrival served us cooked meats and sagamity. My men, who had not had any sagamity for over a year were delighted with this reception, to which they did great credit, consuming large quantities of this liquor.[71]

These savages tried in every way to persuade me to pass the night in their village. They said that a short distance from their settlement there were four white men, who sold them cloth, blan-

[70]If Milford had traveled from the "caves" exactly opposite to the compass direction he gave, he would have passed through Oklahoma, Arkansas, and Missouri, crossing the White near its headwaters to reach the Missouri River in the western part of the state (i.e., Osage Indian country), which is much more reasonable than marching off in impossible directions from which he could never have gotten back to the Creek country.

[71]"Sagamity is a beverage made from cornmeal."— Milford. It was also eaten thick as a porridge.

kets, and other commodities that they showed me. I surmised that these white men were Englishmen from Canada, and I learned later that I was not mistaken; for I did not see them, not having accepted the proposal made to me to remain overnight in the village. I expressed my very warm thanks to these Indians, returned them their weapons, and continued on my way to the Missouri River. On the banks of that river I found a sufficient number of canoes to carry all my men over to the right bank where there was a beautiful prairie with a plateau on which we passed the night. We left next morning at daybreak.

After we had gone through a wood and had left it about five leagues behind us to the west, we recrossed the Missouri River and regained the left bank. We resumed our journey and, after marching for about fifty leagues along the river, we came to a forest where my scouts, to my great surprise, found two white women whom they brought to me. They were rather good-looking, which at first made me think they were foreigners. I asked them where they lived; they indicated the direction to me. I ordered them to go on ahead and show us the way. When we were in the forest, we ran across a little stream flowing in a northwesterly direction, and by following its course we arrived, after an hour's march, at a rather pretty village where these white Indians lived. When they spoke to me, I thought I recognized the harsh language of Lower Brittany. They showed me some sort of books that were written by hand in their language. I asked them for one and in return gave them a little hatchet, which seemed to please them immensely. I have since shown this book to some Europeans, who found that it was written in Welsh. An English scholar told me that, in fact, one reads in the history of England of a Prince of Wales who emigrated with seven or eight hundred families and took refuge in this country. Probably these are descendants of these Welshmen. As I did not understand their language, I was unable to learn the name of their settlement.[72] I left them that same day and recrossed the Missouri River for the third or fourth time and took a northeasterly course. After sev-

[72]According to Welsh legend, Madoc, Prince of Wales, in 1170 sailed west and discovered a new land. He returned home, fitted out a new expedition, and sailed away, never to return. The first discovery of a tribe of "Welsh" Indians (Tuscarora) was announced in 1730; many other tribes were later so honored. Linguistic investigation has disproved the claims. An able summary will be found in Hodge, *Handbook of North American Indians*, II, 931–932. Bernard Romans, discussing the origin of the American Indians, held that "Mr. Powell's story of Maddock the Welshman's voyage, cannot be thought fit, to ascribe a Welsh origin to the savages . . . yet even this has been made use of by a certain Dutch writer, whose name I do not now recollect" (*History of East and West Florida*, 49).

eral days march I arrived at the Mississippi River just where the little nation of Kakias lives, which showed me that I had gone down too far to the east. I had to retrace my steps to the west, where I ran across a then-existing tribe called the Ançalagresses, which is now totally extinct. I also found a portion of the Missouris who had settled on the banks of the river, as well as several other Indian tribes of which I shall not bother to speak because, since the Acadians arrived in this part of America, they have all united and now form only one tribe.[73]

The Acadians have settled at New Madrid, which was given to them by the Spanish Government. Banished to France when Canada was conquered by the English, these Acadians arrived at New Orleans in 1785 after long tribulations. The Court of France had obtained for them from the King of Spain some land on the right bank of the Mississippi at the point called The Fork, not far

[73]By "la petite nation de Kakias" Milford could mean Kaskaskias or Cahokias; some of these Illinois Indians had moved over the river to Missouri. The Ançalagresses are so extinct as not to be identifiable. I suggest that Milford derived this hitherto unrecorded tribal name from *Anse-à-la-Graisse*, the popular name for the place where New Madrid was founded! There were Missouris living within a hundred miles to the west of St. Louis. What the Acadians had to do with all this only Milford knows. It seems odd that the travelers should miss all the towns of the Illinois Country, west and east.

from the Ohio River, where they now are perfectly happy. They are industrious, but lack incentive, because they have an abundance of everything and are under the domination of the Spanish, who do nothing to rouse them from their torpor. However, if they should become French citizens again, they would engage in trade and would profit greatly from their present advantageous situation. The winter here is extremely severe, but they know how to provide for their needs during this season when they neither hunt nor fish. They ordinarily while away the time by fetes.[74]

The King of Spain sent engineers to New Madrid to draw up the plan of a new town, which should be the most beautiful in the universe if it is built according to these specifications.[75]

---

[74]What basis Milford thought he had for this account of the Acadians it is impossible to say. Following an agreement between the French and Spanish courts in 1785, arrangements were made for the transportation of certain Acadians from France to Louisiana (Kinnaird, *Spain in the Mississippi Valley*, II, 127–131). They were not, of course, the first Acadians to go to the Mississippi; the earliest had reached that haven in 1768. They could not have been sent to New Madrid, for there was no town of that name until 1788–89. The Fork at which the Acadians were settled was not that of the Mississippi and the Ohio, but La Fourche Bayou in southern Louisiana. Could he possibly have meant the town of New Iberia, Louisiana, which was existing as a settlement by 1785?

[75]The city was planned on magnificent lines by George

After a six days march we came to a little river called the St. Francis. We lay down on its banks, but it was impossible to sleep because of the enormous quantity of water-fowl of all kinds, which made an insupportable racket. We continued our journey and after a day and a half came to the Missouri River and soon afterwards to the fort built by the Spanish at the junction of the Missouri and the Mississippi at 38° 36″ north latitude.[76]

The river is sheer mud. Its course, which I followed for about seven hundred leagues, flows from the west-northwest with an astoundingly rapid current. There are now very few Missouris. They live in a little wood thirty leagues below the point of confluence of this river with the Mississippi. All the barter commerce with the tribes I encountered along the Missouri is in English hands. They come up by way of the

Morgan, its founder; the colonizing scheme fell through, however, and the place never flourished. See Savelle, *George Morgan, Colony Builder*, 212–213; Houck, *The Spanish Régime in Missouri*, I, 302–306.

[76]The St. Francis River rises about sixty or seventy miles south of the Missouri River and flows south to enter the Mississippi more than fifty miles below Memphis. Having marched from a spot on the Missouri not far from its mouth, Milford reaches the St. Francis after traveling for six days, and then one and a half days later he arrives at the confluence of the Missouri and the Mississippi.

lakes, setting out from Quebec or Trois Rivières
where they obtain the merchandize they trade
for peltry. The Spanish, envious of this commerce, built the fort of which I have just spoken
so as to keep the English from passing, but the
latter, whilst they were with the Indians, built
rafts or very flat boats. They stowed their most
valuable peltry in the middle and that of less
value on the sides to serve as protection and in
this way passed the Spanish fort. They had to
sustain some cannonades, but they were rarely
hit because of the extremely rapid current. They
had a trading post on the opposite bank where
they deposited their merchandize and were safe
from the Spanish, who made no attempt to trade
with all these savage tribes. This trading post is
now a pretty little town half a league below the
confluence of the two rivers.[77]

  We crossed the Mississippi and next day in the
afternoon came to the Ohio or Belle Rivière.[78]
We then returned to that part of our territory
called the Yazoo Country, where our hunting
range is located; from there we went to the
Chickasaws and the Cherokees. We next de-

  [77]Can he mean Cahokia on the left bank about twenty
miles below the Missouri?
  [78]If they traveled from the mouth of the Missouri, they
made excellent time in reaching the Ohio the next afternoon, since that would have been a hike of more than one
hundred and thirty miles.

scended the Coosa River and arrived back home eighteen months after our departure, having traveled twenty-six hundred leagues without losing a single man and without any accidents or illness, bringing with us about five hundred horses laden with the most valuable peltry. In addition, each of my warriors had a small bundle of beaver and otter skins of his own. All were extremely satisfied with their journey, and their families were very delighted to see them again.

As I had sent a messenger to the nation to notify them of our imminent arrival, the people came to meet us from all the villages along our route and gave feasts in our honor. In every village my warriors had several relatives or friends who immediately joined us, so that on arrival at my habitation (which I had named *Petit Paris*) my band was augmented by more than two thousand persons who remained with us for three days while we took the war medicine.

According to Creek usage, a savage arriving from a long journey, whatsoever its nature, may not return to his own home till he has been purified by a war medicine. I shall describe this medicine in Part II of this work.[79]

When we had discharged this duty, I sent my warriors home to their families to rest, inviting them to be ready to set off on another expedition

[79]See pp. 171–173, 219–220.

if they were so inclined, and I myself took a rest
for three weeks. As the war between the Anglo-
Americans and English was still going on, I
decided to muster some warriors again with the
idea of making an incursion into Georgian territory. On arriving at the frontier, I gave my warriors orders to abstain from all overt hostilities
and to occupy themselves solely with hunting
till I returned. It was my intention to go secretly
and alone to reconnoitre the French, English,
and American armies, which were then in Virginia. I set out and learned the position of the
three armies; I even went as far as Philadelphia
to see if I could find some French merchant who
would be able to take charge of all the nation's
commerce. My search having proved unavailing,
I rejoined my companions in arms, and we returned to the nation. It was not till two years
later, and in the course of another journey, that I
ran across an English company by the name of
William Panton, John Forbes, and Leslie, who
were entrusted, by treaty, with all the nation's
commerce.[80] These three men, the very soul of

[80]William Panton, born in Scotland about 1745, had
come out to America before 1770. Presently, with John
Leslie and Thomas Forbes, he formed Panton, Leslie and
Company and from 1784 through McGillivray's influence
controlled the Creek trade (Caughey, *McGillivray of the
Creeks, passim*). It was McGillivray, not Milford, who arranged this business.

uprightness, honor, and probity, never abused the nation's confidence in them; on the contrary, they constantly rendered the latter the greatest services. This company is still in existence and enjoys the highest reputation amongst the savages, especially the Creeks. William Panton was my especial friend. He died a short time ago as the result of troubles brought upon him by a scoundrel named Bowles, who, according to an article from New York in *Le Publiciste* of 9 Vendémiaire, Year 11 [October 1, 1802], now styles himself "General of the Indians." The role that today this wretched individual seems to play could prove too disastrous for the French for me not to make a point of showing him up in all his infamy and of revealing the utter perfidy of the Anglo-Americans, whose tool he is.

REGARDING THE PERSON OF GENERAL BOWLES

Bowles is an American; his family lives in Baltimore. At the beginning of the American Revolution he was serving in an English regiment in the capacity of ensign. He was garrisoned at Pensacola a short time before the Spanish regained possession of it under the command of General Galvez. Bowles, after committing several thefts in the regiment, was cashiered by the English; he went to New York where he made every effort to enter another English regiment

(the Royal American), which was garrisoned on
the long island, of which New York is the capital.
However, as they knew all about him, they
would have nothing to do with him. Not knowing
what to do he joined some actors and went to
Providence Island where we shall leave him on
the boards for a moment whilst we relate an
anecdote having to do with Lord Dunmore, his
next employer.[81]

Lord Dunmore was governor of Providence.
William Panton, of whom I have just spoken, was
doing a very big business in peltry and had sent a
schooner with six thousand piastres to his
partner Forbes, who lived in Providence. The
governor, getting wind of it, seized the piastres
on the pretext that this money was contraband.
Panton lodged a complaint in England where
Lord Dunmore was compelled to return the six
thousand piastres. Angered by this sentence,

[81]William Augustus Bowles had come to Florida in 1779
as ensign in a regiment of Maryland Loyalists. Dismissed
at the age of fifteen for a breach of discipline, he had been
befriended by a party of Creeks at Pensacola, lived and
fought with them in aid of the British, and was re-com-
missioned for meritorious conduct at the siege of Pensacola in 1781. On the surrender of that town Bowles was
sent with other British prisoners to New York, but presently obtained leave on half-pay and returned to the Creek
country. Sometime in 1785 he went to St. Augustine and
thence to New Providence (Kinnaird, "The Significance
of Bowles' Seizure of Panton's Apalachee Store in 1792,"
156–192).

Lord Dunmore sought every occasion to revenge himself on Panton's business concern. To achieve this end, this is what he did. There was a very rich man in Providence by the name of Miller who discharged the office of lieutenant governor. The Lord proposed his establishing a trading house among the Seminole-Creeks in opposition to Panton. Having agreed on the ways and means of carrying out the project, their eye fell on the actor Bowles, with whose effrontery they were well acquainted, and sent him to make the initial arrangements on the premises. He embarked on a fishing boat, which put him off on the banks of the Apalachicola River, whence he ascended to the Seminoles and from there to the lower Creeks in the town of Kasihta. From here he sent a band chief to McGillivray with a letter and a little sword mounted in silver on behalf of Lord Dunmore. As Bowles had not revealed his intentions, McGillivray thought the English were getting ready to make war on the Anglo-Americans in favor of the Creeks, and under this assumption would have agreed to Bowles' demands when just then, to his bad luck, I arrived back from an expedition on which I had been absent for some time.[82]

[82]John Murray, Earl of Dunmore, formerly governor of Virginia and at this time governor of the Bahamas (1787–96) and John Miller, a partner in Miller and Bonamy of

McGillivray had written to him several times, asking him to come to see him and give him full particulars of his plans, but Bowles, under one pretext or another, always declined to comply with this request. McGillivray having informed me of the matter, I left at once for Kasihta[83] where I found this man. I stayed with him a week, during which time he told me all about his projects.[84] It was not difficult to see that here I had to do with a man without honor and without probity; but as he claimed to be the emissary of Lord Dunmore, I respected his office and limited myself to giving him formal orders to leave the nation within three days. At the same time I ordered the chiefs of the Kasihtas to cut off his ears and send them to McGillivray if he had not

New Providence, thought they saw an opportunity to cut in on Panton's trade monopoly and hoped to create difficulties between the Creeks and the Spanish. On 22 June 1788, the arrival of "a stranger" (Bowles) was reported; from this moment on McGillivray's skillful management of the whole business is quite clear (Caughey, *McGillivray of the Creeks,* 186 ff.)

[83]The Kasihta town was on the Chattahoochee a little below the Coweta town.

[84]McGillivray sent Milford away with Bowles and John Richmond (secretary to Miller) with instructions to pry out as many secrets as possible. The Frenchman returned from this mission to Little Tallassie on 1 February 1778. It was McGillivray, not Milford, who got rid of Bowles. See the editor's introduction for a full presentation of this matter.

left by the fourth day. Having learned of this, Bowles left at once for Providence, taking with him two Seminoles and three Cherokees.[85] Immediately on Bowles' return, Lord Dunmore sent him off to Canada. On arrival at Quebec he found a ship ready to sail for England and embarked on it with his five Indians. When he got to London he had himself presented to the Minister as the chief of the Creeks and Cherokees.[86]

The English Minister, who knew how vital it was for his country to live on good terms with these savages, had a house placed at Bowles' disposal and assigned him an annual sum for his expenses. Bowles dressed like the Indians to give a semblance of reality to his story. A lady of distinguished family fell in love with him and was on the point of marrying him when she was probably informed of some of the exploits of this adventurer and sent him packing. While in London he invented a fricassée that he called *Fricassée des Cherokees*, which created quite a sensation at the time and was served at the best tables. I only report these details to bear out in particular the truth of my assertions. There is no doubt that Bowles had a great penchant for the stage, for,

[85] "The Seminoles are a separate tribe under the protection of the Creeks. They are nearly all thieves."—Milford.
[86] "I do not know if he went under his own name, but the affair is too recent not to be known."—Milford.

though the Minister treated him with special consideration, this did not prevent his making an arrangement with the directors of the theatre whereby they paid him every time he brought his Indians to a performance. He also took them to Vauxhall where he had them dance. This conduct displeased the English Minister, who made him leave, giving him some old swords and some old pistols to distribute among the Creeks and Cherokees. He embarked on a ship belonging to that same Miller of whom I have already spoken.[87]

On Bowles' return to Providence, Lord Dunmore sent him off again to the Seminoles, this time, however, in company with a score of malefactors who had long been awaiting their sentence in the prisons and one of whom has since been hanged in London. On arriving among the Seminoles, Bowles busied himself with obtaining peltry by fair means or foul. He knew that the honest Panton had a large stock of peltry and other commodities at St. Mark of Apalache and conspired to plunder it. To achieve this end, he collected a number of Seminole Indians to whom he gave different articles of merchandize of little

[87]Panton's summary of Bowles' adventures between incursions has been quoted in the editor's introduction. Bowles' own story as elicited by an English journalist (Benjamin Baynton) was published in London in 1790.

value that he had brought along with him, on condition that they assist him in stealing the merchandize in Panton's store.[88]

To diminish in their eyes the horror of such a procedure, not of course that they were at all delicate in such matters, but because of Panton's fine reputation, he told them that he had come on behalf of the King of England to make Panton & Company pay for the articles transferred to that firm in St. Augustine for distribution to the Indians; that this company had not carried out the King's designs but instead had appropriated these effects without either having paid for them or given any equivalent; that he had come to inform the Indians that, if they wished to follow him to St. Mark of Apalache, all the merchandize in Panton's store would be theirs with the exception of the peltry, which he would be content with as his share.

[88]Bowles returned to the Creek country in September, 1791, giving out the impression that he had "a Commission from Mr. Greenville Secretary of State in England appointing him Superintendant & General, & he tells the Indians that he has Come to rescue them from the americans & from Panton & McGillivray" (McGillivray to Panton, 28 October 1791). Bowles seized the Panton, Leslie store at St. Marks on 16 January 1792. The full documentary story is in Caughey, *McGillivray of the Creeks*, 295–314, and Kinnaird, "The Significance of William Augustus Bowles' Seizure of Panton's Apalachee Store in 1792," 156–192.

Persuaded by this astute reasoning, the Seminoles went along with him and promptly carried out his orders, and in a trice the peltry was transported three leagues away to be shipped on the Ochlockonee River. As soon as I learned what had happened, I went to the Seminoles and took one hundred and fifty men to go in pursuit of this thief and send back all the Seminoles who were with him. He was warned that I was on his trail. Aware of the danger he ran (for I should have hanged him), he decided to write to the Spanish captain, Viegaz,[89] commandant of Fort Apalache, to sue for protection. The captain asked him to come to the fort and explain why he was forced to implore his aid. He did so; and while he was there, the captain received the official report of the theft that he had just committed. Not feeling qualified to pronounce sentence on this affair, he made Bowles immediately embark on the King's schooner and had him taken to New Orleans. Baron de Carondelet, who was governor there, passed him on to the captain-general at Havana, and the latter turned him over to Madrid for trial. Here he was kept in confinement eight years, and it was only after my

[89]Diego de Vegas. However, in 1792 the commandant of St. Marks was Francisco Xavier Guessy. Vegas took over command from Captain Francisco Montreuil on May 16, 1794 (Kinnaird, *Spain in the Mississippi Valley*, III, 295).

return to France that Lord Dunmore, his protector, obtained his release from the Spanish Government.[90]

On coming out of prison, he went back to London where he embarked for Providence; from there he proceeded again to the Seminoles; and I have since learned that he plundered Panton's establishment a second time and that, when the Spanish captain who commanded Fort Apalache tried to prevent it, Bowles blockaded the fort and forced him to capitulate. All the baggage and effects belonging to the King of Spain were stolen by Bowles and the Seminoles under his command. He then went to St. John on St. Mary's River, ten leagues north of St. Augustine in eastern Florida where the King of Spain owned a cattle farm, Panton a trading post, and a number of the inhabitants, horses and

[90]Actually, Carondelet sent Pedro Rousseau and José Hevia to invite Bowles to visit New Orleans under safe-conduct to discuss his proposed treaty between the Creek Nation and Spain. Something of Bowles' point of view (in his self-named capacity of "General and Director of Affairs of the Creek Nation") is expressed in his letters of 13 and 14 March 1792 to Carondelet (Caughey, *McGillivray of the Creeks*, 310–313; Kinnaird, *Spain in the Mississippi Valley*, III, 13–14). For an interesting summary, see Las Casas to Floridablanca, 21 April 1792, in Kinnaird, III, 27–34. Bowles was sent under guard to Havana; he was presently imprisoned in Madrid and later in Manila. While being returned to Spain in 1797 he escaped and made his way (1799) once more to Florida.

negroes. He had everything carried off by the Seminole Indians among whom he is at present living. Panton saw his fortune utterly destroyed by the ravages of this highway robber and was unable to survive the troubles that he brought upon him. Such is this Bowles whom our papers call "General of the Indians" and whom I should have hanged after his theft if he had fallen into the hands of my Indians.[91]

I must here inform the reader that the notice published in *Le Publiciste* of 9 Vendémiaire, Year 11 [October 1, 1802], dated New York, August 7, is not correct; first, because it says that Bowles gave orders to set fire to, or sink, the American ships, and then, because it says that the Governor of New Providence gave pursuit to this Indian pirate.

I ask if it is very likely that this Bowles, a protégé of the Americans and an American himself, would ever dare to do such a preposterous

---

[91]In 1800 Bowles set up his State of Muskogee, captured Fort St. Marks and held it for five weeks; he was taken prisoner in 1803 and imprisoned in Morro Castle, Havana, where he died three years later. Panton died 26 February 1801. Consult McAlister, "The Marine Forces of William Augustus Bowles and his State of Muskogee"; Boyd, "The Fortifications at San Marcos de Apalache," 20–21; Greenslade, "A Journal of John Forbes, May, 1803—The Seizure of William Augustus Bowles." For an excellent summary of Bowles' last adventures, turn to Whitaker, *The Mississippi Question, 1795–1803*, 162–175.

thing and if Lord Dunmore, Governor of New Providence, who constantly makes use of his services and openly protected him in his depredations, would have him pursued.[92]

This article was written at Paris with the object of persuading the French Government that this man has succeeded in having himself named Chief of the Indians of North America and that I no longer have any title to that post. I shall have occasion at the conclusion of this work to tell the government what interest the Anglo-Americans have in thus destroying the government's good opinion of me and how they are afraid that it will employ me and enable me to check their overweening ambition through the power of the savage nations who have often been a source of great anxiety to them, as one shall see.

MCGILLIVRAY IS APPOINTED AGENT OF THE KING OF SPAIN

In 1784 McGillivray and the war chiefs of the Creek nation went down to Mobile to negotiate a treaty with M. Miró, Governor of Louisiana, and the intendant, M. Navarro, of whom I have spoken above, both of whom also went to Mobile for this purpose. It was stipulated that the Spanish Government furnish the Creeks with arms

[92]Dunmore was no longer governor of the Bahamas at the time of the third Bowles affair.

and ammunition whenever they had to make war on their enemies. The two Spanish commissioners then offered McGillivray the title of Commissioner-General to the Indians in the service of the King of Spain, which he accepted with the object of more closely cementing the friendship between the two nations established by the treaty. At the same time they offered me the post of assistant commissioner, which I declined and which I only accepted when Baron de Carondelet assumed, in the name of the King, the post of Governor-General of Louisiana and the Floridas. I filled this post with honor and to the satisfaction of the Creeks and the Spanish Government. Later I shall give my reasons for relinquishing it.[93]

DOUBLE-DEALING OF THE GEORGIANS

When peace with Spain was concluded and the treaty signed, we returned to the nation, but we were not there long before we were compelled to declare war on the Anglo-Americans. Here are the causes that led to this war. Two old band chiefs who had been made micos,[94] Tanquim

[93]This treaty meeting was held at Pensacola, not Mobile, 22 May—1 June 1784; Miró appointed McGillivray "commissary of the Creek nation" 7 June 1784 (Caughey, *McGillivray of the Creeks*, 75–77).

[94] "The Creeks give this name to the old men who in time of peace are charged with police duty. The word

[the Tame King] and Falquim [the Fat King] by name, went to Georgia where some wealthy men of that region, thinking they were powerful kings among the Indians, entertained them and made them drunk, with the express purpose of taking advantage of their intoxication for their own ends. They drew up in writing a considerable land grant and, when the two micos had recovered from their drunkenness, the Georgians presented this document to them, assuring them that they had dictated it. The micos protested against such an assertion, stating that they had no right to cede, or even to sell, this land; that, if the Georgians wanted it, they must address themselves to the assembled chiefs of the nation; that they alone could do nothing in the matter; and refused to ratify this grant by affixing their customary mark.

The Americans, seeing that promises would get them nowhere, resolved to resort to force. They called in several armed men who threatened

means King. I shall go into it in greater detail in Part II."
—Milford. The author reduces the importance of the micos, who were actually the head chiefs of the towns. According to Swan "each town has its chief or *mico* . . . [and] has also what they style *beloved second men*, whose business is to regulate the police of the town and public buildings. They are generally men of the best memories, that can tell long stories, and give minute details of ancient customs" ("State of the Creek Nation in 1791," 279).

to kill the two micos unless they immediately complied with the demand made of them. The latter, finding themselves roughly treated and in imminent danger of losing their lives should they offer any resistance, did what they were asked, and as soon as they got away, reported to the chiefs of the Creek nation the manhandling and violence to which they had been subjected in Georgia by the Anglo-Americans.[95]

It was to prevent the latter from taking possession of this land that the nation declared war on them, which proved costly for them and caused them very keen anxiety. This land is situated between the Ogeechee and Oconee Rivers and measures twenty leagues from east to west and eighty leagues from north to south.

I mustered my warriors and immediately marched against their frontiers. All my engagements were successful, and they no longer at-

[95]Milford is vague about time. The difficulties with Georgia referred to occurred two years after the Pensacola treaty. The Creek point of view is well summed up in letters from McGillivray to Miró (1 May 1786) and to Zespedes (15 November 1786). The chiefs named were the Tame King of the Tallassies and the Fat King of the Cussitahs (Kasitkas) who went to visit in Georgia in the fall of 1786 and were seized as hostages. It is possible that Milford is confusing this with an earlier incident in 1783 when two chiefs of the second rank went to Georgia and under threat of death made an extensive grant of land on the Oconee. Consult Caughey, *McGillivray of the Creeks*, 106–110, 138–140.

tempted to meet us in battle. As they knew that McGillivray was Supreme Chief, the Americans thought it was he who was conducting the military operations, which redounded to his reputation. His name figured in all the newspapers in the United States, and he was servilely flattered on his military exploits, which amused us both immensely. I recall one passage in a paper of that time which said: "How skilfully he conducted this unfortunate war against us! We would be lucky if we could win him over to our side, because then the other Indians would never attempt to wage war against us. Let us then try to make peace with him."[96]

The Anglo-Americans did not have the faintest idea that a Frenchman was leading the Creek army and that McGillivray, who relied entirely on my fidelity and friendship, remained quietly at home. They learned this later. I am now going to relate a little anecdote to show that this estimable man possessed few soldierly instincts. I only mention it because he told it to all his friends, and he himself would laugh over it were he still alive.

One day I persuaded him to come to my camp

[96]The Creek war broke out in June, 1787. On 8 January 1788 McGillivray wrote to Zespedes: "Our operations of the last Six months have provd very favorable to us. My Warriors are Victorious in every quarter over the americans" (Caughey, *McGillivray of the Creeks*, 165).

to witness the operations of the army. While he was there we had a rather sharp encounter with the Anglo-Americans just outside the town Augusta. I was with Colonel Brown, who commanded an English company fighting with the Indians under my command. This is the same Brown who shortly before had received rough treatment at the hands of the Americans. After removing all his clothes they dipped him from head to foot in a barrel of tar and then rolled him in feathers. They sent him off in this condition, and he had to remain that way for several days for fear lest, by going to his friends, he jeopardize their safety. This occurrence came near killing him, and it was to revenge this treatment that he placed himself at the head of the Royalists.[97] Right at the very beginning of the engagement,

[97]There is some confusion here. According to Charles Jones, a Thomas Brown in the summer of 1775 was tarred and feathered by the parish committee of Augusta for his loyalist sentiments. As a British officer he assisted in the capture of Augusta in 1779 and was commandant there until its capitulation in 1781. He was exchanged shortly after (*History of Georgia*, II, 177–178, 335–336, 448–449, 492). This was probably the Colonel Thomas Browne who, after service in the Florida Rangers, was British Indian agent for the southern department, 1779–1783 (Shaw, *British Administration of Southern Indians, passim*). He went to England in 1784 but in 1788 was at New Providence (Caughey, *McGillivray of the Creeks*, 203). There is no evidence that Brown or Browne had a share in the Creek campaign of 1787.

McGillivray hid in the underbrush, where he remained till nightfall. Winter was then coming on, and he began to feel cold; since we ordinarily fought naked, with the body painted in different colors, he was obliged to do the same when he came to the camp so that he suffered greatly from the cold and could do nothing about it till the engagement was over. He then came out of hiding and courageously went on to the battlefield to despoil one of the Anglo-American dead and wrap himself in the latter's cloak. He rejoined me three days later and said that he did not like to witness such affairs, that never again would he be caught in a similar situation, and in fact he left at once. Since then we often laughed over his terror and the Anglo-American's cloak. When one possesses such executive ability and so many fine qualities as Alexander McGillivray, one does not need military virtues to be a great man.

If I still had the sweet satisfaction of counting him amongst my friends, I should find in him a zealous champion with the French Government and all the outrageous nonsense spread abroad about me to bring me into disrepute with the government would vanish into thin air before the language of truth.[98]

[98]He did not always sing the same tune. On 26 May 1793 he wrote to Carondelet: "McGilvrit and I feared each other. I feared him because I knew his spirit and the

CONFEDERACY OF THE INDIANS OF
NORTH AMERICA

When I arrived in the Creek nation, the savage tribes used frequently to war with each other, which facilitated any enterprises that their enemies might wish to initiate against them. I proposed, in a grand war council of the nation, that they put an end to this evil by forming a general alliance with the different Indian nations in this part of the continent. To this end I pictured to the assembled chiefs the inordinate ambition of the Anglo-Americans who encroached daily on the territory of the Creeks and would soon be in a position to crush them if, on their side, the Indians continued to war amongst themselves. I told them that all the red men should unite like brothers against the white men, their common enemy. The assembly perceived the truth of my observations and immediately sent an order to the chiefs of all the neighboring tribes to rendezvous three months later at an appointed place on the Creek frontier for the purpose of holding a grand council. This assembly took place in 1785. It was there resolved that each grand chief

malice of his family, and he feared me because he knew how strong my influence was, being general of the nation and always ready to march at their head whenever it was necessary" (Caughey, *McGillivray of the Creeks*, 358–359).

should inform the individual chiefs of the contiguous nations of the proposed confederation and invite them to form part of it. In the course of the same year, all the savage tribes of North America were leagued together, and the following year they sent chiefs to the grand council of the Creeks, the dominant nation of the confederacy, to receive instructions regarding the national policy during the year.[99]

This confederacy frequently made the Americans quake with fear since more than once they had found how disastrous for them the hostility

[99]An assembly of chiefs of the Creek, Chickasaw, and Cherokee nations was held at Little Tallassie in July, 1785. McGillivray, for them, submitted to the Spanish officials a memorial protesting any claim that the American government might set up for their lands in consequence of the treaty between England and the United States and asking that the Spanish envoy (Gardoqui) enter into no boundary terms unfavorable to the tribes (Caughey, *McGillivray of the Creeks*, 90–93). Whether further action was taken at this grand council looking to close confederation of the nations is uncertain. In March, 1786, McGillivray called an assembly of all chiefs of the Creek nation to discuss the encroachment of the Georgians (*ibid.*, 103–106). On 20 June 1787 McGillivray reported to O'Neill that "we have had a great Meeting with the Chiefs of the Northern Nations, the Chiefs of the Iroquois, Hurons, Mohocks, Wyandots, Oneidas, & Shawnese. They are Sent from the northern Confederacy, Consisting of Twenty five Nations, that Inhabit about the Lakes, River Ohio, Wabash & other parts of the Western Country of North America. I have concluded Matters with them to Serve the Kings Interest. . . ." (*ibid.*, 153).

of the Creeks could be, for they had often been defeated by these savages. It may be recalled that twelve or fifteen years ago the Americans wrote in their papers that they could no longer hold out against the Indians, who made continual incursions into their territory. At that time, the mere name of McGillivray made them shudder, and they often put a price on his head; but it was not easy to seize him. They knew that the esteem and respect he enjoyed among the Indians was grounded on their confidence in him. They resolved to make him lose this, and this is how they went about it.

DEPARTURE OF MCGILLIVRAY FOR NEW YORK. HE IS APPOINTED GENERAL IN THE SERVICE OF THE UNITED STATES.

In 1790 Washington, the President of the United States, sent two American colonels to McGillivray to invite him to come to New York. I was away when these emissaries arrived. McGillivray immediately sent an Indian to notify me that he was preparing to comply with General Washington's request. I was at Pensacola where I was busy distributing to the Indians the presents that the King of Spain was accustomed to give them every year. I replied to McGillivray by the same messenger, begging him not to leave before my return and informing him that it was imperative for me to discuss with him the motives of his journey. He appreciated the justice of my request and had resolved to await my return, when a certain Joe Cornell, an American by birth and his Indian interpreter, informed the two emissaries that, if they waited till the Tastanegy, McGillivray's brother-in-law returned, their journey would prove fruitless, that the latter would never allow McGillivray to go. They profited by this advice and in one way or another brought such pressure to bear on McGillivray that they persuaded him to leave, which he did, with twenty-eight band chiefs, three days before my arrival.[100]

[100]The first step towards this treaty had been the sending of three commissioners (General Benjamin Lincoln, Cyrus Griffin, who had been president of Congress under the articles of Confederation, and David Humphreys, poet and wartime aide-de-camp to Washington) to meet McGillivray and other chiefs at Rock Landing on the Oconee in September, 1789. McGillivray was dissatisfied with the terms offered and rejected the treaty. He particularly objected to the clause that placed the Creeks under the protection of the United States and also to a boundary clause confirming Georgian encroachment on the Oconee. The full report of the abortive commission is in *American State Papers, Indian Affairs,* I, 65–80. The following spring Colonel Marinus Willett as special envoy of Washington came to persuade McGillivray to go with other chiefs to meet the President. In New York on 7 August 1790 McGillivray signed a treaty with virtually the same terms as those previously rejected, except that it apparently contained a secret clause providing for carrying on

I distrusted his weakness and mustered four thousand warriors to await his return at the frontier, but I did not carry out this project. My fears were well-founded, since McGillivray made a treaty with Washington in which he ceded to him a part of the land east of the Oconee River, precisely the same land that the Georgians wanted to take by force from the two micos, of whom I have previously spoken and for which reason we had waged a terrible war with the Anglo-Americans.

This treaty greatly displeased the Indian chiefs, who refused to ratify it; this prevented the Americans from taking possession of the land.[101] It was not till I had returned to France that they ventured to seize it, which was not difficult inas-

the Creek trade through the American ports, should the Gulf towns be closed; and McGillivray did insist that the acknowledgement of American sovereignty applied only to that part of the nation within American boundaries. Twenty-three chiefs signed with McGillivray. After the signing of the treaty McGillivray was unanimously elected (August 16) an honorary member of the St. Andrews Society of New York! (*American State Papers, Indian Affairs*, I, 80–82; Peters, *Indian Treaties*, 38; Caughey, *McGillivray of the Creeks*, 251–254, 256–262, 273–276).

[101]The dissatisfaction was apparently stirred up by the Spanish. The preamble of a treaty between Carondelet and McGillivray (6 July 1792) mentioned "great uneasiness among the different Chiefs of the Nation, the greater part of whom are decided to reject the said treaty with the United States" (Caughey, *McGillivray of the Creeks*, 329).

much as I had forbidden my savages to make war with them whilst I was away, which I did not think would be for long.

In addition, McGillivray had accepted the rank of general in the service of the Americans, which the President gave him out of gratitude.[102] Although he was very fond of me, he feared me even more when he realized that he had done a weak thing; so on his return six months later he was very embarrassed when he told me of his agreement with the President of the United States. At that time he was accompanied by an American officer named Swan[103] who, I believe, is now in Paris and of whom I shall speak very shortly. McGillivray commenced by showing me the presents that the President had sent me with

---

[102]Secret clauses of the treaty apparently provided an annual allowance of $100 each to six chiefs and a salary of $1200 a year to Brigadier-General McGillivray as agent of the United States (*American State Papers, Indian Affairs,* I, 125–127).

[103]Caleb Swan (later paymaster-general of the army, 1792–1809), on orders from Secretary of War Knox, had left New York with McGillivray 19 August 1790 in the capacity of Deputy Agent to the Creek Nation and arrived at Little Tallassie on 8 October. He remained among the Creeks until 17 January 1791. To him we owe one of the best accounts of the Creeks in the late eighteenth century. The man in Paris was James Swan (1754–1830), a Scottish-born merchant who went to Boston in 1765 and to France in 1787, where he was presently an agent of the French Republic.

the order to confer on me the rank of general, if that title were agreeable to me. I returned everything, thanking General Washington for the offer he was kind enough to make me and stating that I could not be in the service of the Americans, of the Spanish, and of the Indians at one and the same time, and that I was content with the latter and the title of commissioner of the King of Spain.[104]

PERFIDY OF THE ANGLO-AMERICANS

Some time later an officer arrived who was charged by General Washington to give McGillivray the pay attached to the rank of general and to me one thousand piastres, though I had not accepted the title proffered me.[105] The money was all in piastres and was loaded on the horses in such a way that, when passing through the town of Oakfuskee, one of the money-bags burst

[104]This story, as well as that below about making McGillivray return the American commission, seems to be pure fabrication.

[105]This officer was Ensign John Heth, acting under War Department orders of 31 May 1791, who carried $2900 to pay the salaries of McGillivray and two interpreters, the allowances of the six chiefs, and the annuity to the nation; the total sum was $3700, but $800 had been anticipated at New York the previous August. Milford's name is nowhere mentioned; no money had been authorized for him (*American State Papers, Indian Affairs,* I, 125–127).

right in the center of town where all the Indians were congregated. The officer did not fail to inform them that this money was destined for McGillivray, knowing quite well the effect this would have on them.

This perfidy, thoroughly worthy of the Anglo-Americans, almost cost McGillivray his life. For the Indians, already very incensed with him on account of the treaty with Washington and the title he had accepted, were now furious and spread the report throughout the nation that their Supreme Chief was a traitor. Several chiefs banded together to go and kill him, but I was warned in time to save his life by promising the chiefs that I was going to take cognizance of the affair. I made McGillivray return to Washington his commission, as I had done; but the Indians were no less enraged at him over the treaty, and in a second assembly that they held they would surely have killed him if I had not made him go to a plantation that he had in Mobile till they had calmed down. Some time later he went to Pensacola where he died in Panton's house, as I have already said, and without his treaty having been ratified by the Indian chiefs.[106]

[106]There is nothing to substantiate Milford's statement that he forced the return of the commission. McGillivray certainly remained head of the Creek Nation until his death 17 February 1793 at Pensacola, where he died in

When he conferred on McGillivray the rank of general in the service of the United States, General Washington, at the same time, made him a present of a very costly pair of epaulettes, which he said had been sent to him by the Court of France and delivered to him by Marquis de LaFayette. McGillivray gave them to me some time before his death.[107] They are the ones that I brought with me to France and that I used for a long time in Paris. As they were very long and differed in form from those that were then worn, I exchanged them for more modern ones such as one wears today.

I have said that, when he returned from New York, McGillivray was accompanied by an American captain named Swan. The reader will not be annoyed if I give some details about this man and Washington's reasons for sending him to the Creeks.

General Washington was well aware that the treaty he had made with McGillivray would be of no service to him till the chiefs of the nation and

Panton's house of "a Complication of disorders of Gout in the stomack attended with a perepneumony." According to Milford (writing to Carondelet 26 May 1793), McGillivray's family was "circulating the rumor that he was poisoned" (Caughey, *McGillivray of the Creeks*, 353-354, 359).

[107]"Our President, whilst *M'Gillivray* was in *New York*, complimented him with . . . the Golden Epaulet which he had worn throughout the War" (Pope, *Tour*, 51).

the elders had ratified it. He sent Captain Swan
to await this ratification and do all that he could
to persuade the chiefs to this end. Swan stayed
six months without accomplishing anything. He
came to see me very often. We went hunting together and sometimes remained away a whole
week. I frequently had occasion to remark how
eager Mr. Swan was to get hold of some good
land; every time we traversed any that might suit
his purpose, he asked me to cede it to him. His
comments in this respect often made us both
laugh. He would have had far more confidence in
any grant from me than from McGillivray, for,
since he was not wanting in intelligence, he had
quickly perceived the authority I had over the
Indians and their confidence in me. He returned
at the end of six months without having obtained
the land grants that he asked of me or the ratification that he anticipated. The Americans, on
finding that they could not obtain possession of
this land, then made up their minds to buy it;
and this is how they proceeded.[108]

FOUNDING OF THE YAZOO, OR SCIOTO, COMPANY

A company was organized at Philadelphia and
in Virginia under the name of Yazoo Company,

[108]Except to show on his map the location of Milford's
house, Swan does not mention the Frenchman in his account of the Creeks.

which placed on sale all the territory of this
name, now changed to Scioto. They issued a
pamphlet in which they offered numerous in-
ducements to purchasers of this land; and to
make it seem legitimate took pains to announce
that McGillivray had a partner's interest in the
project, which displeased him greatly. He found
it very wrong that the Americans were permitted
to use his name to deceive the public in this way.
This was one reason why he decided to return
his general's commission to President Washington, to whom he bitterly complained of the pre-
tended company with which his name had been
associated. I owe it to McGillivray's memory to
state emphatically that he never had anything to
do with the reported speculations in the Scioto
lands and even less with such an absurd company
because he could have sold all this land for the
benefit of the Creeks without the Americans
having any share in it.[109]

[109]"Everybody knows what a noise the sale of the Scioto
lands made in Paris and many other cities in France at
different times."—Milford. In this paragraph Milford
confuses the Yazoo companies on the Mississippi with the
Scioto Company on the Ohio and scrambles the order of
events. The South Carolina, Virginia, and Tennessee
Yazoo companies were formed not after the treaty of 1790
but in 1789 on the basis of grants by Georgia. The companies used McGillivray's name without permission, im-
plying that he was a partner, but he strongly disapproved.
That he wanted no part of them is clear from his corres-

I know that there is now a Mr. Swan in Paris who is made much of by the Anglo-American ambassadors. As I have not had occasion to see him, I cannot say whether he is the person to whom I have reference. I should recognize him in a moment, and if it is really he, he should recall the circumstances of which I have just spoken.[110]

MY VARIOUS JOURNEYS IN THE NATION

When the nation was at peace, I took advantage of it to satisfy my desire to get acquainted with the neighboring tribes as well as the different regions of the North American continent. To this end I took with me several warriors, not only as guides on my travels but for my personal safety. This is one of the journeys I made shortly before I went back to France.

I visited the Iroquois, the Hurons, Lake Erie, Lake Ontario, and the falls of the Niagara River, which represented a distance of five hundred leagues. I went up as far as Lake Superior, two hundred leagues from Niagara and returned to

pondence. "Among other assurances that Colo. Willett was authorized to make me, I found that the overthrow of the associated or Yasou Companys was in my power," he wrote to Miró, 26 February 1791 (Caughy, *McGillivray of the Creeks*, 259–262, 288, 318). For the history of these companies see Haskins, "The Yazoo Land Companies"; Whitaker, *The Spanish-American Frontier*, 122–139.

[110]See note 103.

the Illinois via the Lake of the Woods, a distance of three hundred and fifty leagues. From the Illinois I followed the right bank of the Mississippi down to New Orleans, a distance of five hundred leagues, and from there went to the Creek nation (two hundred leagues), making a total of seventeen hundred and fifty leagues. I next visited the trading post Vincennes, which now belongs to the Americans, who have changed the name to Vincent. It is situated on the Wabash River, a tributary of the Ohio, which in turn empties into the Mississippi near New Madrid where the Acadians are now settled, as I have said above. The inhabitants are French creoles married with Indian women of the Wabash and Miami tribes. They have planted vineyards, but the wine is of no value. I also visited the Osages and came back over beautiful prairies to Chickasaw Bluff near the Wolf River on the banks of which is settled a part of the Chats or Owabenaki nation.[111] Twelve

[111]No confirmation of these travels is possible. We merely note that his mileages are indeed approximate. We might think, too, that, if he traveled down the right bank of the Mississippi, he would have made some comment on passing St. Louis and Ste. Genevieve. A few of the French at Vincennes may have had Indian wives, but not most. Milford could have met Abenakis on this trip; in the 1780's they were living chiefly on the Ohio but in that decade they began to move to Missouri and the Arkansas (Kinnaird, *Spain in the Mississippi Valley*, passim). *Chats* may be an abbreviation for *chatots*; if so, these

years ago I hanged one of these latter savages for killing an American colonel and his son.[112]

When off on these journeys with my warriors, we lived for the most part from hunting. When we had need to re-stock our provisions, I had my band pitch tent, one part going hunting and the other preparing the fires for cooking the meat. I don't know where one gets the idea that these

were not Abenakis but a separate tribe living about this time on Bayou Boeuf in northeastern Louisiana.

[112]Compare Pickett, *History of Alabama*, II, 80–82: A Colonel Kirkland of South Carolina, with his son, his nephew, and several others, after a visit at Little Tallassie in 1788, traveled on to Pensacola with a servant of McGillivray as guide. They were presently ambushed by "a Hillabee Indian, who had murdered so many men, that he was called Istillicha, the *Man-slayer*—a desperate white man, who had fled from the States for the crime of murder, and whom, on account of his activity and ferocity, the Indians called the *Cat*—and a blood-thirsty negro, named Bob." All the white men were killed. "Dividing the booty, the murderers proceeded to the Creek nation, and, when the horrid affair became known, Colonel McGillivray sent persons in pursuit of them. Cat was arrested; but the others escaped. Milford was directed to convey the scoundrel to the spot where he had shed the blood of these men, and there to hang him, until he was dead. Upon the journey to that point, Milford kept him well pinioned, and, every night, secured his legs in temporary stocks, made by cutting notches in pine logs, and clamping them together. Reaching the creek where poor Kirkland and his men were murdered, Cat was suspended to the limb of a tree . . . . While he was dangling in the air, and kicking in his last agonies, the Frenchman stopped his motions with a pistol ball."

Indians eat their meat raw. I can certify that they eat it better cooked than in any country in Europe. The only difference is that they often eat it without bread, but this is due more to circumstances than to their natural taste. They are very fond of dipping their meat in bear grease or oil after it is cooked. They often carry this grease along with them in bamboo canes prepared especially for this purpose.

On the banks of the Ohio or Belle Riviere I found a species of vegetable, the roots and stalks of which are very similar to those of the carrot. It is a very subtle poison. One day I came upon seven of the men known here as frontiersmen because they have no fixed habitation and spend all their time in the forests. Six had just died from eating this carrot, and the seventh, who was still alive, suffered frightful cramps, though he assured me that he had barely tasted it. I had my men carry him to our camp, and there I wanted him to take some bear oil, but he was unable to swallow it. He was at the point of death when the thought struck me to squeeze out some plantain juice and have him take it. He had no sooner drunk this liquid than he felt better. I gave it to him several times, and within a very few days he was completely cured. He then returned to Post Vincennes to report the death of his companions.

One finds in the Ohio a soft shell turtle, the skin of which is as soft as linen; the flesh is very delicate and palatable. There is also a great quantity of excellent fish in this river. In its vicinage I discovered quite good-sized coal and lead mines; the Indians make use of the latter.

During the twenty years that I spent among the Indians I often made these journeys; and though I did so solely for my personal gratification and not with the intention of describing them to the public, they none the less enabled me to learn the traits and manners of the nations that I visited, the products of their lands, and the way to get along with them and gain their confidence, a far from easy thing to do.

I TENDER MY RESIGNATION AS COMMISSIONER
OF THE KING OF SPAIN IN ORDER
TO GO TO FRANCE

I had been about twenty years in the Creek nation when, at the beginning of the French Revolution, Spain declared war on France.[113] I learned of the revolution through the United States papers, but their reports varied so greatly and were so contradictory that I could not be sure of anything. When I heard that Spain had declared war, I feared that if hostilities extended to the

[113]The French Republic declared war on Spain 1 February 1793.

colonies I should be obliged, as agent of the King of Spain, to aid him against the French. In order not to be reduced to this extremity or to betray the confidence of the King of Spain, I tendered my resignation to the Spanish Government, stating that as a Frenchman I could not remain in its service.[114] At the same time I requested it to send me a passport for England since I was afraid I should meet with a refusal if I requested one for France. I also asked for a document certifying to my loyalty to the Spanish Government. I waited eighteen months for these papers; they were finally sent to me by the Governor of Louisiana, Baron de Carondelet. The following is a copy of his letter to me in this connection:

New Orleans, January 14, 1795.

I have received, sir, the several letters that you have addressed to me, etc. . . . I am accordingly forwarding you the passport you requested, as well as a detailed certificate of your services, which I hope will meet with your satisfaction. Although it is no longer so easy as heretofore to recompense and oblige the persons who are of service to His Majesty, I have arranged for you to be paid a gratuity of three hundred piastres for your voyage, which I hope will be a very happy one. Be careful not to run into a priva-

[114]As late as April, 1794, and possibly throughout this year, Milford was acting as a temporary Spanish agent to the Tallapoosa Creeks (Kinnaird, *Spain in the Mississippi Valley*, III, 288).

teer, which, taking you for a refugee, might give you very rough treatment.

> I have the honor to remain, sir, very sincerely
> Your very humble and very obedient servant,
> Baron de Carondelet

P.S. If I failed to reply to your previous letters, it was because I knew you were not in Pensacola.

My passport, my commission as chief of the Indians, and the certificate are deposited in the offices of the Minister of Foreign Affairs in Paris.

In the interval between my application for the passport and its receipt, I drew up a memorandum setting forth the potential advantages to France of the retrocession of Louisiana by the Spanish, who have derived few advantages from it because the Indians do not like them. I offered the alliance with the Creeks, the most powerful Indian nation in North America, which for this reason would bring with it an alliance with all the other tribes. I asked France only for a few men and no money, and I guaranteed success.[115]

MY ARRIVAL AT PHILADELPHIA AND
MY DEPARTURE FOR FRANCE

When I had completed my plan, I chartered at my own expense a ship on which for eighteen

[115]Perhaps this was a draft of the "Memoire Présenté par François Tastanegy, Grand Chef de Guerre de la

thousand, five hundred francs I went to Philadelphia to see the French Ambassador, Citizen Fauchet, now Prefect of the Var.[116] I informed him of the motive of my voyage; he approved of my projects and assured me that they would be acceptable to the French Government. He urged me very strongly to go to France, gave me a passport, and offered me passage at government expense on board a vessel that was about to sail for Bordeaux. I accepted the passage that he offered me, but I did not wish it to be at government expense. I paid my passage; I considered such a sacrifice very slight if it were of advantage to my fatherland. Compared with those that I had recently made, the journey was indeed prompted by my desire to serve my country, for I voluntarily relinquished my post as commissioner of the King of Spain (which was worth three thousand, five hundred piastres a year to me, a sum that I never even had the time to spend) and that of Grand War Chief of a nation whose esteem and confidence I had earned and that was disposed to do everything for me.[117] In fact, I did not leave

Nation Crik. Au Directoire Exécutif de la République Française. En l'an Cinq." See the editor's introduction.

[116] Jean Antoine Joseph Fauchet (1761–1834) arrived in Philadelphia in 1793 as minister plenipotentiary to replace Citizen Genet and served there until July, 1795. He was made prefect of Var in the year VIII (1799–1800).

[117] Milford was not Spanish Commissary to the Creek

without acquainting it with my plans and without assuring it that I should return when I had obtained for it the alliance with the French.

MY ARRIVAL IN FRANCE

Accordingly, I arrived in Paris with the recommendations of Ambassador Fauchet 9 Thermidor, Year 3 [July 28, 1795]. I presented myself to Citizen Cambacérès, now one of the Consuls and at that time President of the Committee of Public Safety. He received me courteously and sent me to Citizen Treilhard, then secretary of the committee, who informed me that they could not comply with my request because they were negotiating a treaty with Spain and I must wait till this treaty was concluded so that the government might know what course it should pursue. In the year 4, that is, about six months later, Citizen Charles Lacroix, at that time Minister of Foreign Affairs, presented me to the Directory, which approved my plans and directed the ministers of the Navy and Foreign Affairs to concern themselves at once with how best to obtain from the Court of Spain the retrocession of Louisiana. When I was assured of the success of my project,

Nation either before or after McGillivray's death; he was not on the Spanish payroll before May, 1792, at the earliest; and his pay was no more than five hundred piastres (Caughey, *McGillivray of the Creeks*, 338, 359; Kinnaird, *Spain in the Mississippi Valley*, III, 178).

I indicated to the government my desire to return to America because I had no means of livelihood in France. The Directory replied that it was necessary for me to remain in France till the government could put my proposed plans into execution; and to make it possible for me to remain, it passed a resolution 6 Germinal, year 4 [March 27, 1796] conferring on me the rank of brigadier general with the pay attached to that rank, valid both in France and the colonies. I have that decree in my possession; I enjoyed the benefit of this arrangement up to 1 Vendémiaire, year 9 [September 22, 1800].

For seven years I have been awaiting, with all the confidence that the Government of France must inspire, the fulfilment of the promises made me in its name. As long as I knew that it was impossible to carry them out, I voiced no protest; but now that it is making ready to take possession of Louisiana and put into effect the plan that I submitted to it, and for which reason alone I came to France, I should be indifferent to the interests of my country, to those of the Indians on whose behalf I came, even to my honor, if I did not remind the government of its obligations to me. I have too much confidence in its loyalty not to be convinced that it will put aside for a moment my enemies, who are even more its enemies, to take cognizance of my reclamations.

I admit with all the candor of my soul that, if my seeming oblivion at this time were injurious only to my own personal interests, it would concern me very little; but I know too well the nature of my enemies not to be aware of the length to which they will go to gain their ends. I have told in the course of this work how greatly the Anglo-Americans fear the Creek nation; I have also said that their overweening ambition tends to nothing less than to dominate the entire American continent and to drive out all the European powers that have colonies there. Here is the place to draw attention to the influential role they played in the war of Santo Domingo and Guadeloupe, for all the while their warships were cruising in American waters more pertinaciously than the English, the President, Mr. Adams, maintained a consul at the Cape, which Toussaint most certainly would not have tolerated if a plan of independence for this colony had not existed between this general and the President of the United States. There can be no doubt whatever that their ambition leads them to look upon the West Indies as an appendage of their continent. The aid that these colonies, in time of war, are obliged to demand from them strengthens them in this idea. In fact, during the last war, Santo Domingo and the other French islands procured from the United States the provisions and other necessities that they could not obtain from the mother country. It is therefore essential, as I have said before, that an European power establish there a military force that commands respect more through its geographical situation and its connections with the different Indian tribes of America than through the number of its soldiers. The retrocession of Louisiana can give France such a position. The Anglo-Americans appreciate so keenly the importance of this retrocession that they are ready to make any sacrifice in order to hinder it; and if they cannot hinder it, they seek at least to diminish its advantages by preventing a man already known to, and loved by, the Indians, a man who could immediately win their support for France, from appearing in their midst. The Americans know perfectly well that, if the French Government should place it in my power to carry out the plans that I have submitted to it, their projects of expansion would straightway vanish and the Creek nation, which they have taken upon themselves to civilize, would become for them a Medusa's head. They go to any length to discredit me with my government; they represent me as a mere cipher, without abilities of any kind. They announce that I have no ascendancy over the Indians, that I am not their chief, and that they are at this moment under the authority of General Bowles, who, as I have said, takes great care not to leave the Seminole nation and is as much a general of the Creeks as Mandrin was a general of the French when he was on the frontiers of Savoy. Nevertheless, however persistently they try to disparage me, I will at least be fair enough to admit that in so doing they are endeavoring to serve their country. It is for the French Government to distrust them. In this regard I rely entirely on its foresight and justice.

PART II

PART II

I TOLD in Part I of my departure from France, of my arrival in the United States of America, and later in the Creek nation; then of my travels amongst the various allied tribes. In Part II I shall describe the character of the tribes I visited, illustrate by anecdote their customs and way of life, and tell of the rivers, the provinces, and their different products.

ARRIVAL AT NEW LONDON

I said in Part I that I departed from France in January, 1775, and disembarked at New London in April of the same year. This town offered nothing of interest; its inhabitants have little education but they are quite industrious. They raise fruit and vegetables on the land in the vicinity of the town. They have a very large quantity of apple and pear trees, from the fruit of which they make fairly good cider, which they sell, along with their vegetables, in Virginia, the two Carolinas, Georgia, the Bahamas, and even as far as Santo Domingo. I stopped only a short time in this town and, since I shall have little occasion to speak of it again, I am going to relate an incident that took place there in 1786, which illustrates the ignorance and simplicity of the inhabitants.

A large part of the inhabitants of New London are members of the New Lights. A ship's captain who was out of employment took instruction in this sect, and the preachers delegated to catechize him told him in their teaching, the purposive aim of which was to enable him to achieve the grace of extraordinary prayer, that, if he attained such perfection through the power of his faith, the gates of New Jerusalem would be opened unto him and, having in this world achieved the perfection of the saints, he would no longer be subject to resurrection and the last judgment but would immediately partake of the joys of the Heavenly Kingdom.

This man, who was probably unaware that they were speaking figuratively, took everything they told him literally and resolved to enter New Jerusalem at once. To this end he suggested to several of the Awakened as credulous and as ignorant as himself that they build a fast sailer and he would take them to New Jerusalem; in this way he would enable them to avoid the unpleasantness of dying and of awaiting resurrection. They believed all he said and clubbed together to provide the sum necessary for the construction of the ship. The women donated their rings, their earrings and other jewellery; the men gave money, and those who had none went out into the forest to cut down and bring in the timber necessary for the ship. When the vessel was completed and ready to sail, the captain was in a very great quandary to know which direction to take. In order to extricate himself from this dilemma, he conceived the idea of telling the passengers that, since the prospective voyage was a very long one, it was prudent and, in fact, indispensable for their safety to try out the ship first. All his associates, admitting the truth of this, decided to freight her with a cargo of cabbages, carrots, onions, cider, and other products of the district, which the captain took to Cape Français and with which he did a very profitable business. The voyage took three months at the end of which time he brought back in exchange a cargo of rum and molasses, which pleased the owners of the ship immensely, since they were very fond of both these products. On his return the captain announced that during the voyage he had learned that New Jerusalem was an imaginary, chimerical place and for this reason he could not undertake to conduct them there. At the same time he turned over to them his new cargo, which in appealing greatly to their palates easily consoled them for this non-fulfilment of their hopes. They agreed to let the captain keep the ship on condition that from time to time he fetch molasses for them.

I myself did not witness this incident, because I was then in the Creek nation, but I read about it in an American paper that appeared at the time.[1]

NOTE REGARDING THE AMERICAN, ARNOLD, AND THE DEATH OF MAJOR ANDRÉ

I left New Orleans [i.e., New London] to go to Norwich, the home of an American named Arnold, who at the beginning of the American wars made some noise in the world. I shall not pass on to other topics without giving some details regarding his conduct, which caused the death of Major André.

At the outbreak of the American Revolution, Arnold was a horse dealer in the United States and at the same time a captain of the militia. He performed several fine exploits at the beginning of the War of Independence, which redounded to his honor and through which he hoped to be appointed commander-in-chief. When he saw that Washington was preferred to him, he grew so jealous that he forthwith formed the project of

[1]There had been many New Light Baptists in New London since 1740. The reference to the New Jerusalem, however, suggests the Swedenborgian Church.

revenging himself. To achieve this end, he entered into correspondence with the English General Clinton and promised to deliver over to him the fort guarding the entrance to the province of New Jersey. The English general thereupon sent Major André to him to look over the ground and take with him the proper measures to ensure the success of the enterprise.

The Major, assuming that Arnold had taken every precaution to conceal his designs, went to him with confidence, but as he was leaving, he was arrested. Arnold immediately fled and reached the river where some sailors were awaiting him. He had them take him to the English general in New York who, to requite him for his treason and to profit by his knowledge of the American defenses, conferred on him the rank of general in the service of the King of England, while Major André paid with his head for his confidence in Arnold.[2]

I TRAVEL THROUGH THE DIFFERENT COLONIES OF THE UNITED STATES

On leaving Norwich, I went to Providence, to Newport, and to Boston. I have mentioned in Part

[2]Benedict Arnold, born in Norwich, 1741, was a druggist and bookseller in New Haven at twenty-one. He presently invested in the West Indies trade, selling horses and mules to planters in the sugar islands. The fort guarding the "entrance to New Jersey" was West Point.

I that there is a great antipathy between the inhabitants of the northern and the southern colonies. In fact, they are remarkably jealous of each
other, and I think this is traceable to the religion
of the Quakers, which forbids them to employ
negroes for the cultivation of their land and thus
greatly reduces the advantages they might derive
therefrom. As they are very avaricious, they are
extremely envious of their fellow countrymen who
augment their riches by means of negro labor. The
Quakers have a species of hog of astounding size,
as big in fact as our European donkeys. They
breed a very large quantity of them, as well as
cattle, which they salt and then sell in the West
Indies.

From here I went to the long island, of which
New York is the capital. The inhabitants of this
island, who are nearly all of Dutch extraction, are
very affable and hospitable. They are courteous
to foreigners, but they were swindled so often by
the Europeans during the American war that they
got the idea of adopting this policy themselves,
with the result that today one must beware of
having any dealings with them.

I have noticed that in North America nearly all
the land situated on the seaboard is quickly worn
out. In the west, this condition extends fifty to
sixty leagues inland. For this reason the Americans never have land enough, and this is why the

inhabitants of this vast territory abandon their land and go west to drive out the Indians and take theirs. On my arrival in this country, Kentucky still numbered only four [*sic*] inhabitants, who lived in cabins like those of our charcoal burners; but the population has increased so greatly through the aforesaid emigration that today they are in a position to muster an army of sixty thousand men. Kentucky adjoins Cumberland, which has been populated in the same manner and to an almost equivalent extent.[3] These two new colonies of the United States can scarcely tolerate their union with the Anglo-Americans, and since they are self-sustaining, they are only awaiting a favorable occasion to detach themselves entirely from the Congress. They already elect their governors without the intervention of Congress or the Senate. They possess excellent land with inexhaustible resources. I stayed only a few days in New York and from there went on to Baltimore, passing through Philadelphia and traversing an extensive tract of country covered with wheat.

At Baltimore I embarked for Yorktown in Virginia[4] where I stopped only a short time, going

[3]In 1800 the population of Kentucky was 220,000 and of Tennessee, 105,000.

[4]"I have noticed that in this country tobacco requires the ground to be renewed every year in order not to

from there to the two Carolinas. North Carolina is very sandy; here they raise rice, maize, and large crops of potatoes, from which the inhabitants make a sort of rum that they call whisky. This liquor, which they distil badly, usually has a very disagreeable smoky taste. One finds here also a large quantity of peach trees, from the fruit of which they make a very good brandy. When it is carefully made and has been aged for four or five years in a wine vault, it is as good and as delicate as the best French brandy. They also raise indigo, but it is of poor quality. The products of South Carolina, of which Charleston is the capital, and where I only stayed a few days, are approximately the same and of a little better quality.

THE REASON FOR THE RAPID POPULATING OF GEORGIA

From Charleston I went to Savannah in Georgia. About ten leagues up the river of the same name, one finds very large rice plantations. When I arrived in this district, I found few inhabitants; now it is very densely populated. Here is how this came about.

In 1784, the date of the American peace[5] and

degenerate. The Virginians neglect to do this, which greatly lowers the price of their tobacco."—Milford.

[5] 3 September 1783.

the independence of the Americans, there were a very large number of dishonest vagrants in the United States, the inevitable outcome of a revolution, of which they are a direct product and at the conclusion of which they should be put out of the way.

Peace having deprived these outlaws of the means of livelihood that they had found in the devastation and evil abuses inseparable from war, the lives and property of peaceful men were daily exposed to danger. To rid themselves of this scourge, the latter leagued together and declared war to the knife against all these vagabonds who could not overcome their habit of plundering. Finding themselves thus energetically pursued, they were forced to seek another refuge. They retired to Georgia where no one interfered with them; but as they cannot get over their long continued practice of thieving, they often go to the backwoods of the two Carolinas and Virginia and carry away from the unfortunate inhabitants all the horses they can lay their hands on. This is the reason for the rapid populating of Georgia, which, as one sees, does not make for very pleasant neighbors.

I went up the Savannah River as far as Augusta, which was then only a small village and today is quite a large-sized town. I crossed the river to go to Orangeburg situated on the outskirts of South Carolina, and from there I proceeded in a westerly direction as far as Tugaloo, of which I have spoken in Part I.

NOTE ON THE AMERICANS CALLED
CRACKERS OR GOUGERS

I also wrote in Part I that in visiting Tugaloo, Franklin, and other places in the interior of the United States, I came across a special type of Anglo-Americans known as Crackers, or Gougers, who are nearly all one-eyed. I was curious to know the reason for this. The reader will perhaps not be displeased if I here report what I learned on the spot.

The reader will recall my having said that the inhabitants of North Carolina raise a large quantity of potatoes from which they make a sort of rum that they call whisky. These Crackers are very fond of this liquor. Since by nature they are quarrelsome and wicked, after drinking it they wrangle among themselves and agree to fight it out on an appointed day. Their fights are very like pugilism or English boxing, except that they are more murderous. When the Crackers have settled on a day and hour for a fight, they collect all the spectators they can and arrange them in a circle, with themselves in the center; then at a signal given by the oldest person in the crowd, the fight begins.

It is well to note that these men, from childhood on, take great care to let their finger nails grow and never cut them. In order to make them very hard, they frequently soak them in tallow and then hold them over the fire; the tallow, in melting, penetrates into the pores of the nail and makes it exceedingly hard when it is dry. I have seen some here that are as hard and dangerous as the claws of a lion. Not content with this weapon, they also wear spurs (the rosette of which is a very sharp spike), which they never remove even for sleeping. It is with arms such as these that they present themselves for the fight. It is easy to see how deadly they are.

When the old man has given the signal to begin by saying: "Anything goes," the two adversaries violently attack each other with their teeth, spurs, and finger nails, in the use of which they are very adroit. When one of the two falls, the other takes full advantage of the opportunity to lacerate him cruelly from all sides and easily manages to gouge out an eye. Up to this point, the crowd watches the combat with the greatest apathy; not till then does it call off the fight, and if this does not take place promptly, it sometimes happens that both eyes are torn out. The victor mounts a stump, a large number of trees having been cut off about three feet from the ground, and there, covered with blood, he gloats over his victory, insults the crowd, and challenges one spectator after another, saying that there is not a man among them who can touch him. Anger so enflames his imagination that, if no one presents himself to demand vengeance for his insults, he defies the Master of Breath to come down from heaven and stand up against him. When he is done with all his provocations, he gets down from the stump, and everybody applauds him and proclaims him victor. As these fights take place frequently, one finds very few men in this nation who have not been blinded of one eye in this manner.

These men are very evil and do not want to submit themselves to any authority; for the most part they live only by hunting. They plant a little tobacco, which in winter they take to the maritime towns and trade for whisky, fire arms, and gun powder. Although I only stayed a few days with them, I still had occasion to be invited to a meal, the oddness of which amused me enormously; the food, however, was very bad. And here's the reason for it.

One of these men, recognizing me as a foreigner, invited me to dinner, together with several of his countrymen. His wife, who had heard that one took tea in good society, asked her husband to get her some in exchange for tobacco, and he brought her half a bushel. She put the entire quantity in a pot along with a large ham, and then boiled them together till the ham was cooked. When the guests arrived, she put the ham on an earthen plate, threw away the liquid, placed the tea leaves on another plate, and then served them at table. I saw all the faces beam at the sight of a *ragout* that they thought was going to be wonderful, and each prepared to enjoy himself. I took it all in without saying anything, being in no hurry to be the first to express my opinion of a dish that I knew was uneatable. I watched them lustily chewing their tea leaves (which by no means have a pleasant taste) when on a sudden the woman flew into a rage and threw a plate at her husband's head, reproaching him with having put the money for good tea in whisky and with having fobbed her off with refuse instead. This ludicrous quarrel made me roar with laughter, but it was by no means easy to make the woman listen to reason and grasp the fact that one does not use the tea leaves, but the infusion, mixed with a little sugar.

As I had eaten nothing and was very hungry, I decided to taste the ham, which was quite good, the tea having given it an excellent flavor. I ate a lot of it, seeing that this was all there was.

These men go almost naked. They are so lazy and addicted to drunkenness that the women have to do everything. These wear a few more garments than the men. In winter they spin cotton and flax, which they combine to make a fabric that serves for their clothes and even for their chemises. The women are as industrious as the men are indolent.

The farther one penetrates into the interior of the United States, which is settled almost everywhere by the same type of men, the more wicked and dangerous they are. They often kill travelers to strip and plunder them. Even their next-door neighbors are not safe. They go to those who they think have a little money, and when they once succeed in getting in the house, they kill everybody they find, lead away the cattle, and carry off all the movable property, which they then sell in another province. These outlaws wear their hair very close cropped and paint their bodies and faces in different colors, like the savages, so that their appearance is really terrifying.

Every colony of the United States has a governor who, once in saddle, considers himself an absolute sovereign. He employs every means in his power to insure the adherence of the persons under his jurisdiction, impunity being one of his most successful mediums. Thus it is very difficult to obtain restitution of the stolen property from these thieves, of whom I have just spoken, who place themselves under the protection of one of these governors. The demand is often made without success.[6]

DISHONESTY OF THE AMERICANS

I have traveled through the sixteen colonies of the United States of America, and everywhere I went I found false and hypocritical men who never say what they have in mind, who are proud and arrogant in prosperity, vile and abject in adversity. The Americans think they are the salt of the earth; they are so dishonest that they sell land that does not belong to them to several different persons at the same time. I have witnessed this myself in the backwoods of Georgia where I have seen several buyers present themselves to take possession of a piece of land to which they each held equal title.

I have said in Part I that the Anglo-Americans flatter themselves that they will soon be powerful enough to be the sole masters of the entire American continent. The expansion they have achieved within a very short time should most certainly attract the attention of Europe, which cannot too soon set bounds to their ambition.

I left the vicinage of Tugaloo to go to the Creek nation. I traversed immense forests and

[6]For a lively account of backcountry people and ways shortly before the Revolution, see Hooker, *The Carolina Backcountry—The Diary of Charles Woodmason.*

sometimes what looked to me to be very fertile land. The greater part of this is covered with extraordinarily large and lofty trees. Many of them are fruit-bearing, but since I was unacquainted with the fruit, I did not venture to taste it; and besides, since I had my own provisions with me, I was not pressed by hunger, as was later the case.

MY ARRIVAL IN THE CREEK NATION

At the end of several days' march, I came to a river that I later learned is called the Ogeechee.[7] I swam it with my horses, and when I was on the other side I found sandy ground and a forest of firs, some of which were resinous, others with a white wood of bad quality, while others still had a yellow wood that is excellent for masts. I continued in the same southwesterly direction with the aid of my traveler's compass.

As mentioned in Part I, after a journey of about thirty-five days I arrived in the village of Coweta just when the nation was holding its grand assembly.

I am now going to tell the reader something about these assemblies of the Indians, along with

[7]If, after leaving Tugaloo, he crossed the Ogeechee, he must have traveled south for about an hundred miles. If he was traveling southwesterly, it is more likely that he crossed the Oconee, as he reported in Part I.

a brief description of the place where they are held.

When the savages hold an assembly for any reason, before taking up any business, they always first smoke their pipe and drink a beverage brewed from the leaves of a plant that is very common here and is said to be a wild tea plant. It greatly resembles those in China except that the leaf is very much smaller. This plant is green all year round. The leaves are not gathered till one is ready to use them. When the savages wish to utilize them, they parch them like coffee. This is how they prepare the beverage that is drunk at an assembly. They put a certain quantity of these tea leaves into an earthen pot, which they place over the fire. When they are parched to the proper degree, they pour water on them in proportion to the quantity of leaves and then boil the whole. When they think the infusion is strong enough, they pass it through a basket in the form of a strainer and let it cool in special large pots. When it has cooled off to the natural heat of milk, one of the elders in charge of this ceremony has it put into gourds with an opening at the top about two inches in diameter. It is served in these gourds, which are passed in turn to each member of the assembly.

When I was taken to one of these assemblies for the first time, I, as a stranger, was one of the

first to whom they passed the gourd, inviting me
to drink. Although I was absolutely ignorant of
the significance of such a ceremony and the nature of the beverage that was being offered me, I
did not venture to show any distrust and tried it.
Finding that it tasted like tea without sugar, I
drank a considerable quantity of it. Shortly after
the entire assembly had partaken of this beverage,
I noticed that the Indians vomited it very easily
and without the slightest effort. This spectacle,
which by the way was exceedingly disgusting,
made me a little uneasy, and I began to fear that
it was medicine and that I had no doubt taken
far too large a dose. McGillivray, noting my amaze-
ment, asked me in English why I did not follow
suit. I replied that, as yet, I felt no inclination to
vomit, that very likely the physic would operate
in a much more natural way. He repeated my remark to the assembly, which greeted it with peals
of laughter.[8]

---

[8]The "Black Drink," made from the leaves of the *Ilex
Cassine*, the strong infusion of which is purgative, vomi-
tive, and diuretic. Swan noted that the Creeks believed it
"purifies them from all sin, and leaves them in a state of
perfect innocence; that it inspires them with an invinci-
ble prowess in war; and that it is the only solid cement of
friendship, benevolence, and hospitality. . . . a stranger
who goes among them cannot recommend himself to their
protection in any manner so well as by offering to partake
of it with them as often as possible. . . . It is generally
served round . . . three times at every meeting. . . . Their

This ceremony, which at first seemed ludicrous to say the least, is nevertheless grounded on the following very wise principle, which would not always be amiss in the councils of civilized nations. The Indians, as we have seen, discharge this drink very easily and via the same channel through which they take it. But the purpose of this revolting ceremony is to assure the chief of the assembly that each and every member of it has an empty stomach, a resultantly clear head, and that all questions will be debated in cold blood and not under the influence of liquor.[9] The truth of this will be clearly proved in the following description of these assemblies.

The reader will recall that, when I met the

---

mode of disgorging, or spouting out the black-drink, is singular, and has not the most agreeable appearance. After drinking copiously, the warrior, by hugging his arms across his stomach, and leaning forward, disgorges the liquor in a large stream from his mouth, to a distance of six or eight feet. Thus, immediately after drinking, they begin spouting on all sides of the square, and in every direction; and in that country, as well as in others more civilized, it is thought a handsome accomplishment in a young fellow to be able to spout well" ("State of the Creek Nation," 266–267). Bartram (*Travels*, 448–451) too, describes this cassine drinking at some length. See also Hodge, *Handbook of North American Indians*, I, 150; Swanton, "Religious Beliefs and Medical Practices of the Creek Indians," 539–544.

[9]"The Indians are very fond of strong liquor and this practice was adopted to make sure they were sober."— Milford.

savage who introduced me to the Creek nation, I was so nearly famished that I was on the point of killing one of my horses for food and that this old man, far from giving me something to satisfy my hunger, offered me only a slice of watermelon and then escorted me to an assembly, which had convened just at the time of my arrival.

I did not remain long at this assembly, which was of no interest to me at that time. My host took me back to his house and offered me about an ounce of bread and an equal quantity of roast meat, with a glass of water, giving me to understand that this was all he wished me to have for the time being. One can easily imagine that, ravenous as I was, it did not take me long to eat what he had given me. As the day was closing in, the good old man thought I probably had need of repose. He conducted me to a little detached house, to which all my equipment had been brought, and showed me to a room in which I found a bearskin spread out. He indicated to me that this was my bed and thereupon left me.

Although I had not eaten in proportion to my appetite, I nevertheless felt very much better, and since I needed rest as much as food, it was not long before I fell asleep. It is a rather common observation that matters that have occupied our thoughts during the day are retraced in the imagination during sleep. Since I had been nearly

starved and had gone to bed with an appetite far
from satiated, I dreamed only of meals and ban-
quets, to which I did full credit. I was thus de-
lightfully occupied when my host came to ask
how I had passed the night. He brought with
him, in the greatest secrecy, a bottle of rum, of
which we each took a tiny nip; and he then hid
it amongst my things, for fear lest the other Indians should see it.[10]

I AM ADMITTED TO THE GRAND ASSEMBLY

I got up, and he invited me to follow him. We
went a second time to the assembly in the Grand
Cabin, where I occupied the place assigned me
the night before. The entire assembly, recalling
my anxiety regarding the beverage I had drunk,
were still heartily laughing over it.

Before passing on to other things, I believe I
should tell how the Indians conduct their assemblies and give a brief description of the place
where they are held.

DESCRIPTION OF THE SITE OF THE NATIONAL ASSEMBLY

The national assemblies are generally held in
the principal town. A perfect and very large square

[10]"I have already said that the savages are passionately
fond of strong liquor. If a member of any assembly has
any, no matter what kind, he must share it with the others
or else hide it so that they will not steal it from him."—
Milford.

is blocked out in the center of the town, and three cabins of different sizes are erected in each angle of this square, making twelve in all. There are four entrances leading to the center of the square, and the several cabins communicate in such a way that one can see from one of them into all the others. Each of them can accommodate from forty to sixty persons.

That of the Grand Chief of the nation faces the rising sun to indicate that he must always watch over the interests of the nation. Alongside this cabin and in the same angle is the one called the Grand Cabin, where the general assemblies of the nation are held. In the opposite angle there are three other cabins; these are the cabins of the elders and face the setting sun to indicate that they have reached the decline of life and need no longer go on the warpath. In the two other angles are the cabins of the different chiefs of the nation. These are larger or smaller, dependent on the rank of the latter and the services they have rendered.

All these cabins are painted red with the exception of the three facing the setting sun, which are always white, symbol of virtue and old age. In time of war, the cabins painted red are embellished, by way of decoration, with several wooden slats, supporting a sort of chain of wooden rings. This has a sombre significance and apprises the warriors that the fatherland has need of them and that they must be prepared to march at the first signal. In time of peace these chains are replaced with ivy garlands. The three cabins of the elders are always decorated with these ivy garlands mingled with flowers.[11]

As the square on which these cabins are situated is very large, the inner quadrangle is also very large, the reason for which the reader will shortly see.

DESCRIPTION OF THE GRAND ASSEMBLY

I have already said that the chiefs of the nation must assemble every year in the month of May to hold a grand council and discuss there all affairs, domestic as well as foreign, of interest to the nation. When they are all congregated at the rendezvous called the Grand Cabin, of which I have just spoken, the council is constituted, and after

---

[11]Milford is describing the square at Coweta. According-ing to Hawkins the mico of the town with the counsellors and the second men occupied the building facing east; the warriors' cabin faced south; the cabin of the beloved men north; and the cabin of the young people and their associates west (*Sketch*, 69–71). Swan reported that the cabin of the first men of the town faced west, of the warriors north, of the second men south, and that the fourth (facing east) housed the apparatus used in cooking the black drink ("State of the Creek Nation," 264–265). Bartram described in detail the square at Tukabahchee and its buildings (*Travels*, 452–455).

it is constituted no member may leave the enclosure till all the business of the nation is concluded. The president alone is permitted to absent himself for a brief period, but he is obliged, like all the rest, to pass his days and nights in the assembly and to be present at all the deliberations.

While the assembly is in session, no one may come within twenty paces of the Grand Cabin. Only the warrior chiefs are admitted here. The subordinate chiefs present are there to wait upon the others, but they have no voice in the deliberations. The women are charged with the preparation of the necessary food and drink for the assembly; they bring the provisions and put them down at the designated distance; the subordinate chiefs go to fetch them and in turn place them in the Grand Cabin for the members of the assembly.[12]

[12]Milford's "Grand Cabin" is not one of the buildings of the square but, according to Swan, stood at the northwest corner of the square. Hawkins named it "the rotunda, or assembly room, called by the traders, 'hot-house' " and described the construction of one in detail (*Sketch*, 71–72). Bartram said "the great council house or rotunda, is appropriated to much the same purpose as the public square, but more private, and seems particularly dedicated to political affairs; women and youth are never admitted; and I suppose, it is death for a female to presume to enter the door, or approach within its pale" (*Travels*, 448).

In the center of the quadrangle formed by the cabins a fire is kindled which burns continually. At sundown the young people of both sexes congregate and dance round this fire till an appointed hour. During this time the assembly adjourns, and each member, if he thinks fit, betakes himself to the cabin allocated to his rank; or else he remains in the Grand Cabin to enjoy the dances and diversions of the young folk, but without being permitted to leave the quadrangle till all the business of the assembly has been transacted. When the dances, which may not last beyond a stipulated time, are over, each of the members, if the business of the assembly is not too urgent, lies down in the cabin appertaining to his rank; but at the break of dawn, a drum summons all the chiefs to the assembly, which remains in session till sundown.

In entering this assembly, to which I was only admitted because I was a foreigner and a Frenchman (I shall explain later why my being French gave me such a high standing in the opinion of these tribes), I saw at once that McGillivray was chairman of it, but it did not occur to me that he had any other title, so that I asked him several times where the king of the nation was and if he would be present. He laughed at my question and to satisfy my curiosity pointed to the aforesaid three white cabins filled with old men and said: "There are our kings." Then, taking me by the hand, he led me to them. Having been informed of my arrival in the nation, they received me very kindly and had me sit down in their midst, saying: "Welcome, Frenchman! We are glad to see you. As we are very old, we are calmly awaiting death. The Great Master of Breath has not permitted it to occur till our wishes were fulfilled. Since the French departed from these lands, you are the first to visit us, though we have always greatly longed to see them again. The Great Master of Breath, through your presence here, has filled our cup with happiness to the brim."

After this speech, which McGillivray translated to me, there was a long silence. An orator stationed himself in front of me and delivered a harangue that lasted nearly an hour. I frequently caught the word *foulantché*, which in the Creek language means *French;* and each time the orator paused, all the assembly said *ka*, signifying *yes*. And when he had finished his discourse, all the assembly said *mado*, which means *very good*. Next, all the elders lined up in single file and marched past me, shaking hands with me in token of friendship and offering their tobacco pouch for me to take a pinch. After repeating this ceremony with each one in turn, I had so much tobacco that I had to put it in my hat. When the procession was over, one of the elders came up to me and, handing me a tobacco pouch made of swan's skin, made me a present of it.

It is well to note that among these tribes almost all these ceremonial acts have a symbolical meaning. The pouch that this old man presented to me was white, an emblem, as he gave me to understand, of peace and friendship. One proof of the red man's desire not to dip his hands in the blood of a Frenchman, their chosen friends of old, is that they have never forgotten that the French were the first white men they saw in this part of the world. All this was repeated to me in English by McGillivray, since I did not understand a word of the language. But for me the reassuring and even very gratifying thing about it was that it was impossible to mistake the evidences of interest and friendship I received, which seemed all the sweeter and more astonishing in view of their unexpectedness after the description given me by the Georgians and the Crackers, who had depicted these people to me as man-eaters.

It was around midday, and I saw the chiefs being served with cooked meats, bread, and sagamity, a very popular beverage with them.[13] As

[13]"Sagamity is a fermented drink made of cornmeal, which after boiling has an agreeable flavor rather like cider."—Milford. "The common food of the Creek is

my appetite was just as keen as ever, this sight pleased me enormously. After the reception I had just received, I was looking forward to being invited to the meal and was ready to do full justice to it, when my host came and took me by the hand to escort me to his house. I admit that this contretemps distressed me greatly, and I began to think this man intended to make me die of hunger. However, I could not refuse to obey him. So I went along with him, albeit reluctantly. When we got to his house, he gave me a little glass of rum, which I drank; but he did not take any himself, which vexed me. His not doing as he had the night before even worried me a little.

I was enduring the pangs of hunger with great impatience when I caught sight of a table set out with bread, rice, potatoes fried in oil, poultry, venison, beef, and an excellent roast turkey hen. Such an enormous quantity of food made me think my host was expecting a large company,

Indian corn, pounded and boiled, with which they mix a small quantity of strong lees of the ashes of hickory wood. It is boiled until the corn is tender, and the liquor becomes as thick as rich soup. The lees give it a tart taste, and preserve it from souring by the heat of the climate. From day to day they have it constantly standing in large pots or pans, with a spoon in it, ready for use. It is called by the Indians Oafka, and by the whites, *Thin-drink.* Those who have been long used to it are excessively fond of it" (Swan, "State of the Creek Nation," 274).

and I was annoyed not to see anyone as yet, when
he told me in his language, and motioned to me,
to sit down and drink and eat as much as I liked,
that I need not fear the results. He also gave me
to understand that the fast he had made me un-
dergo was based on his fear lest, not having eaten
for so long, the first food would make me ill if it
were not taken with precaution; that now his entire house was at my disposition for as long as I
desired to stay, and that he had given orders to
that effect.

I took advantage of this good savage's generous
arrangements and remained with him a week in
order to rest from the fatigue of the long and
arduous journey that I had just made and that I
should never have undertaken had I known how
difficult it would be. At the end of this time, we
left, McGillivray and I, to go, as I have said before, to his plantation situated near the former
Fort Toulouse. It was while en route that he persuaded me to settle in the nation, where I remained in uninterrupted happiness for twenty
years. I am now going to give the reader an idea
of the traits and customs of the Creek nation.

The Creek nation is composed of a large number of nations, which have joined it and which it
has adopted, but the major part of which have
retained their own customs and language. I am
speaking here only of the dominant nation.

CHARACTER AND CUSTOMS OF THE CREEKS

The Creeks are of moderate height and are of
a reddish copper color; they are strong and robust and easily support fatigue. They are very
great walkers and sometimes march three to
four hundred leagues on their hunting expeditions. They were formerly wicked and cruel
but are now brave and docile if one does not
force them to depart from this character. They
have no definite religion; although they recognize the Great Master of Breath, they have no
religious ceremonies.[14] Every year, in August,
each family comes together to celebrate the Har-
vest Festival, at which time they renew everything that has served them during the past year.
The women break and smash to pieces all their
household appliances and replace them with new.
This is the day that they eat, for the first time,
the new corn and that the priest or medicine man
of the district kindles the new fire and admin-
isters the new war medicine to all the assisting
men.[15] The Indians observe this ceremony so
religiously that those among them who have no

[14]But John R. Swanton contributed to the *Forty-Second
Annual Report of the Bureau of American Ethnology* a two-
hundred page paper on "Religious Beliefs and Medical
Practices of the Creek Indians"!

[15]"I shall describe this medicine later in this work."—
Milford. See pp. 171-173.

old maize to subsist them till this time would eat
roots rather than touch the new maize. This is
also the time that they forget and forgive all their
past enmities. Any Indian who, after the festival,
should renew a former quarrel would forfeit the
good opinion of all the others.[16]

When they go on the warpath, they observe a
very rigorous discipline. The moment they draw
near the enemy they march in single file, with
the chief at the head and each man walking exactly in the footsteps of the person in front of
him. The last in line even sometimes covers up
the footprints with grass. In this way they prevent the enemy from knowing how many of them
there are. When they halt or pitch camp, they
sit cross-legged in a circle, each with his gun
beside him, leaving a passage only wide enough
to admit a single person. The chief sits facing

[16]The festival of the New Fires or Corn Ceremony
among the Creeks is commonly called the Busk. Swan
credited his account of a four-day busk to "Anth[ny]
Alex. M'Gillivray" ("State of the Creek Nation," 267–
268). Hawkins described an eight-day busk at Cussetuh
(Kasihta) (*Sketch*, 75–78). "This happy institution of the
Boos-ke-tuh," he wrote, "restores man to himself to his
family and to his nation. It is a general amnesty, which
not only absolves the Indian from all crimes, murder only
excepted, but seems to bury guilt itself in oblivion."
Swanton treats the subject at great length in his "Religious Beliefs and Medical Practices of the Creek Indians,"
546–614. Bartram also reported the ceremony (*Travels*,
507–508).

this entry to the circle, which no soldier may leave without his permission. When it comes time to sleep, he gives the signal, and from then on no one moves. They are also awakened by a signal.

The dispositions are ordinarily designated by the Grand Chief,[17] who also posts the sentries charged to watch over the safety of the army. There is always a large number of scouts as van and rear guard, so that it is extremely rare for an army to be taken by surprise. With the Europeans, on the contrary, the Indians wage a war of surprise, which is very dangerous for those who are not versed in it.

THE CREEKS ABANDON THE CUSTOM OF BURNING THEIR CAPTIVES ALIVE

When I arrived among the Creeks, they still had the horrible practice of burning their captives alive. I had no trouble in persuading them that such a custom made them odious to all civilized people and that there was a more human and advantageous way of profiting from these captives. I proposed to them that they rate a captive at three scalps[18] and that he was to remain the property of his captor till he was ex-

[17]So Milford wrote, but he meant the Great Warrior or War Chief, not the mico.

[18]"I shall explain later [pp. 173–175] what these scalps are and what value the savages attach to them."—Milford. Bartram, however, years before Milford, reported

changed or ransomed. This advice was approved and adopted by all the chiefs of the nation. It is with men such as these, easy to lead, though intrepid warriors, that I marched against the enemies of the country and with whom I often sowed terror among the Anglo-Americans.

I have said that it was in May, 1780, the time of the general national assembly, that the war chiefs of the Creeks proposed my name to this assembly for the post of Tastanegy or Grand War Chief, which McGillivray had declined. When I had been proclaimed Grand War Chief, the assembly, before adjourning, occupied itself with my inauguration, which was a very long and a very extraordinary ceremony. I shall now proceed to describe it to the reader.

MY INAUGURATION AS GRAND WAR CHIEF

A portion of the assembly came to my house, and when all had arrived, one of the elders had me get up on a sort of litter covered with a bear skin, hung with garlands of ivy, and carried by four band chiefs. When I was seated on this litter, they set out to return to the Grand Cabin. The following order of march was observed.

that "the most ancient traders, both in the Lower and Upper Creeks, assured me they never saw an instance of either burning or tormenting their male captives; though it is said they used to do it formerly" (*Travels*, 211).

Several young warriors, each carrying an eagle's tail mounted on a stick,[19] marched in dancing rhythm, making contortions and uttering hideous yells. They were preceded by a master of ceremonies who carried a cocoanut fastened to a stick; inside this were some seeds, and he beat time by shaking it. In addition to this a young savage at his side gave the beat with a sort of tabor. Marching in front, behind and on each side of my litter, were some old band chiefs, each of whom also carried an eagle's tail, one half of which was painted red. Next came six priests or medicine men,[20] who wore two raw deerskins over their shoulders in the form of a chasuble and carried in one hand a swan's wing and in the other the plant employed to make the war medicine which is taken during this ceremony.

When we drew near to the Grand Cabin, the procession halted. A priest came out to meet us,

[19] "The Creeks or Muscogulges construct their royal standard of the tail feather of this bird [the painted vulture], which is called by a name signifying the eagle's tail: this they carry with them when they go to battle, but then it is painted with a zone of red within the brown tips; and in peaceable negotiations it is displayed new, clean, and white: this standard is held most sacred by them on all occasions" (Bartram, *Travels*, 149).

[20] "Since the Indians have no religious ceremonies other than taking the war medicine, which is made by a sort of medicine man, the latter therefore takes the place of priest in the nation."—Milford.

escorted by two young warriors, each of whom carried a large gourd with an opening at the top large enough to insert a hand. These gourds were painted red and contained water and some juice of the plant of which I have just spoken. This priest stopped about twenty paces from us and, there dipping his hands in this water, aspersed us, meanwhile chanting a hymn or invocation to the Genius of War. When he had finished, all the chiefs who were awaiting us in the Grand Cabin came out to meet us, marching six abreast. When they reached this priest, they dipped their hands into these gourds and moistened their faces; then the six priests who were behind me advanced to them and with one hand laid the plants they were carrying against their faces and with the other passed the swan's wings over them as though to wipe them dry. As soon as the chiefs completed this ceremony, they returned to the cabin, and when they had all gone in, the six priests or medicine men resumed their places behind my litter, and we all proceeded there together. The elder who had placed me on the litter came at once to help me get down and seated me on a buffalo skin which had been spread out for this purpose. Then the whole assembly drank cassine, the tea-like beverage, and for twenty-four hours partook of nothing but this war medicine.

Although I had been appointed Little War Chief and had commanded in the capacity of Grand Chief, I had not yet taken this medicine because I had been careful to make a special one of my own, for it is essential to have one in order to gain the confidence of the savages. This time, however, I had to do as the assembly did and drink the regular medicine. It was not long before I felt severe pains in my heart, which compelled me to disgorge all the medicine I had taken and in this wise to imitate the assembly. This very nauseating ceremony lasted till sunrise. Then the entire assembly stripped themselves, and we all went, absolutely naked, to a circular cabin where the priests were awaiting us. Each of these had brought with him the brass cauldron in which he had brewed the war medicine. Shortly after this, the subordinate chiefs brought some stones, which they had made red hot in the fire in the center of the quadrangle; and the priests, singing all the while, poured over them the water in the two gourds of which I have already spoken, which produced a terrific heat and steam. The entire assembly was perspiring heavily, and my whole body was bathed in such profuse sweat that, though of very robust health, I was afraid that I should not be able to stand it. We remained about half an hour in this state; then some of the chiefs left the cabin, the priests surrounded me, and we all went out and plunged at once into a river a short distance from the cabin. It was not without great apprehension that I decided to imitate the others in this; it seemed to me highly dangerous, sweating as I was, to plunge immediately into cold water; but it was impossible to do otherwise, and I got off with a good fright. However, I still think the purging I had undergone as a result of taking the war medicine prevented the ill effects of such a bath. On coming out of the water, where we remained only a short time, we all dressed and returned to the Grand Cabin where a magnificent repast awaited us. The young people then had permission to come into the quadrangle of the Grand Cabin to dance round the fire, which burned continually throughout this three day ceremony, during which time no member of the assembly might either leave the quadrangle or sleep. It was all the more imperative for me to remain with the assembly since the ceremony took place solely on my account.

I was seated in a distinguished place with the priests on either side. When I happened to get drowsy, one of them dashed fresh water in my face, and the other rubbed it with some pebbles that he had taken care to place for this purpose in the water alongside me.

When the three days were over, I was escorted

back to my house in the same manner in which I had been brought to the Grand Cabin. When we arrived there, the oldest chief announced my appointment and informed me that I was now the foremost sentry of the nation at whose voice the young warriors would be ever ready to march; that the tests through which I had just passed were intended to show me that nothing should abate my zeal and that I should support, with equal courage, cold and heat and hunger to defend the interests of the nation. When the old man had concluded, the assembly broke up, and each person returned to his own home.[21]

I remarked in Part I of this work that the old chiefs had often spoken to me of their ancestors, of the expeditions they had made and the battles they had had to wage before the nation came to settle in its present territory; that the history of these early Creeks, which were then known as Muskogees, was preserved in strands of beads or chaplets, but that, not understanding their arrangement, I had asked one of these elders to recount the history to me in detail. I am now going to relate, as exactly as possible, the narrative told me by this old man.

[21]This all sounds very much like the purification ceremony in the winter-house before the departure of a war party, as set down by Adair (*History of the American Indians*, 167–169).

HISTORY OF THE MUSKOGEES, NOW CALLED CREEKS

After the Spanish conquest of Mexico, all the world knew that this beautiful land of North America was inhabited by a docile and peaceable people who, ignorant of firearms, were easily subjugated. They had only courage and numbers to oppose to the deadly weapons of their enemies; in short, they were defenseless. For what availed bows and arrows against the artillery of an army, weak indeed in numbers, but inured to war, intrepid, and led on by an insatiable greed of gold, which this too trusting people had been unfortunate enough to parade before their eyes?

Montezuma then reigned in Mexico; finding that he was unable to check the progress of the Spanish, he summoned to his aid the tribes contiguous to his dominions. The Muskogee nation, now known as Creeks, which formed a separate republic in the northwestern part of Mexico and had a formidable number of warriors, offered him assistance, an assistance that would have been redoubtable for any but a disciplined army such as that of the Spanish under Hernando Cortes.

The courage of this martial people only served to effect its speedier destruction and could not save Montezuma, who lost his life, and his empire, which was almost totally depopulated. After the death of Montezuma and several other chiefs, the Muskogees, considerably weakened by this dreadful war which they were no longer in a position to wage, chose to abandon a country that offered them in exchange for their past happiness only the most terrible slavery and to seek another that would ensure them the ample resources and the peace and tranquillity of which the Spanish had just despoiled them.

They directed their march northward and within a fortnight had mounted as far as the headwaters of the Red River, in other words, a distance of about one hundred leagues. This river pours its waters across vast prairies in the northern part of America, a fact that decided them to follow its course. They marched for another week in this direction, traversing a prairie studded with the most beautiful flowers and swarming with wild animals, which offered them everything necessary for their sustenance. This region would have attracted them in view of its varied riches, but still fearing for their safety in a region that offered them no natural defenses, they continued their journey.

In their different excursions along this river they never came across another stream, not even a small tributary.[22] But they found many lakes and ponds, some of them with salt water. These

[22]Most of the affluents of the Red River enter from the left (north) side.

were usually teeming with waterfowl of every kind, in particular those birds found on the seaboard. The prairies were alive with partridges, hares, rabbits, turkeys, and other wild life. In these regions the game is so abundant that, when it is hunted from different points at the same time and is forced to flee, it darkens the sky and shades all the ground.

After marching for several days, they came to some clumps of trees where they made a halt. Young warriors were sent out in different directions by the elders to explore the territory. At the end of a month, they returned to report that they had discovered some fine subterranean dwellings along the Red River on the fringe of a forest. The entire nation set off at once, and when they arrived at these caverns, they found that they had been made by bison or wild steers and other animals, which had occupied them because the earth there was a little salty.[23]

[23]Albert S. Gatschet in 1888 (*Transactions St. Louis Academy of Science*, V, 34) ridiculed Milford's story of a Muskogee migration as baseless—as it probably is, historically and ethnologically. The point is, however, that Milford did not fabricate it, for others of his time related similar tales. Hawkins reported that the Creeks had a tradition of coming from "the fork of Red river, west of the Mississippi" (*Sketch*, 19, 81–83). Swan also noted a "general belief" that the Creeks came from the northwest ("State of the Creek Nation," 259–260). Milford seems merely to have embellished a tale he was told. Swanton

The Muskogees found in this region a tranquillity of which they had need in order to retrieve the heavy losses suffered in the Mexican wars. The colony, having brought along its little remaining stock of maize, planted it at once to assure a means of sustenance. As they lacked the necessary implements for working the ground, they used sharp flint stones instead of hatchets to cut and sharpen sticks of wood, which they then hardened in the fire and used for tilling the soil. After this preliminary work in their new settlement, they marked off a field large enough to supply the general needs of the colony and fenced it round with stumps and stakes driven into the ground to prevent incursions by bison and other wild animals, which are very fond of Indian corn. They next parcelled out, by families, the ground in this enclosure and sowed it for their sustenance. The young people of both sexes toiled together in the field, whilst the old men smoked their pipes. They thus passed several years in perfect peace, living by hunting, fishing, and from the produce of their land, regretting

("Social Organization of the Creek Confederacy," 33–75) discusses at length the native legends dealing with Creek history. The Aztec portion seems to be found only in Milford. The caverns of his version are probably literal interpretation of the opening of the oldest extant version (1735) of the migration legend: "At a certain time the Earth opened in the West, where its mouth is. The Earth opened and the Cussitaws came out of its mouth, and settled nearby."

little their native country where they had suffered such adversities. They would, no doubt,
have remained here permanently if the unfortunate fate that seemed to dog their steps had not
compelled them to migrate again.

They were discovered by the Alibamus, who
killed several of their people. So the elders, the
natural chiefs of the nation, called together the
young warriors and sent them on the trail of the
assassins, but without success, because there was
no coordination in their operations and they
lacked a chieftain. They therefore perceived the
urgency of appointing one. The elders of the
nation met together and, choosing the one among
them who had rendered the greatest services to
the country, made him their Tastanegy or Grand
War Chief. His mission was to direct all military
operations, take all necessary measures to avenge
an injury inflicted on the nation, and defend its
rights. He was invested with sufficient authority
for this purpose; but this authority, which made
him the first sentry of the state, the father, shield
and buckler of the homeland, only lasted so long
as the danger. Once peace was re-established
and the troops had returned to the bosom of the
nation, he became again a private citizen and
was only the chief soldier.[24]

[24] "The Tastanegy or Grand War Chief at first took no
part in internal administration: his authority lasted only
so long as the war. But today he is the head chief of the

If he had given no occasion for complaint during the exercise of his authority, he always retained the right to resume his post as soon as necessity arose; and for that very reason, it was incumbent upon him to watch continually over the public safety and apprise the peace chiefs of any injuries inflicted on the nation or of anything that might disturb its tranquillity. When he had announced the necessity of mustering the warriors, a club was immediately exposed in public, part of which was painted red, which meant that a portion of the nation, that is, the young men, must be prepared to march. For if the whole club had been painted red, the entire nation would have had to hold itself in readiness, something that happened only in exceptional cases. Even today the manner in which the club is painted indicates to each special chief how many men he must bring to the appointed

nation both for civil and military affairs."—Milford. According to Hawkins, the Great Warrior of a town decided on war, though the mico and his counsellors could interpose. If the war leader persisted, he walked out of the council followed by those who wanted war. Peace, however, was always determined and concluded by the mico (*Sketch*, 72). The change described by Milford was brought about by McGillivray, Swan reported, who, in order to carry on the struggle with Georgia after the withdrawal of the English on the close of the Revolution, placed "warriors in all cases over the micos or kings" ("State of the Creek Nation," 281).

rendezvous so that the Grand War Chief always knows exactly how many soldiers he can count on, a number that he determines according to circumstances and over which he exercises absolute control.[25]

When it is necessary to order the warriors to rendezvous at a given place, the Grand War Chief distributes to each subordinate chief a club partially painted red. This is generally accompanied by a given number of little wooden sticks which serve to indicate to the warriors who carry them to the different districts of the nation the day they must appear at the general rendezvous with the required number of young warriors. Each day, at dawn, they throw away a stick, and the day they throw away the last one should correspond with their arrival at the rendezvous. There have been few cases of delay in the general muster. In order to prevent any slip of memory, the bearers of the red club are obliged to give the password daily to each chief, this being usually the name and date of the rendezvous. I am

[25]Hawkins wrote, however: "It is seldom a town is unanimous, the nation never is; and within the memory of the oldest man among them, it is not recollected, that more than half the nation have been at war at the same time; or taken, as they express it, the war talk" (*Sketch*, 72). Milford at all times implies a close organization of the military, but no other contemporary source confirms him, just as none support his claim to be commander-in-chief of the armed forces.

now going to give a more detailed description of this red club, tell how it is distributed, and what its purpose is.

Before the Indians were acquainted with firearms, they used only arrows and clubs in their combats. They have now entirely abandoned these weapons, but they have retained the club, solely as a sign of war, and have replaced it in battle with the tomahawk or little hatchet.

When the nation is forced to go to war, the Grand War Chief, or Tastanegy, has a club, partially painted red, exposed in the public square. He also sends one to each band chief, along with a bundle of sticks equivalent to the number of days this chief may take to arrive at the rendezvous. The Grand Chief alone has authority to fix this day.

Each band chief, as soon as he receives the club, has a drum beat in front of the Grand Cabin of the town or village where he lives. All the inhabitants proceed thither immediately; he notifies them of the day and place where he must kindle his fire. He goes to this place before daybreak, lights the fire by rubbing together two pieces of wood, and lays it in the center of a square marked off by four stakes and just large enough to hold the number of warriors that he desires to muster.

At break of day the chief, holding a bundle of

sticks, takes up his position between the two
stakes facing the rising sun. Each time a warrior
comes into the quadrangle, which has only one
place of entrance, he throws away a stick and con-
tinues thus till they are all gone, which represents the number of soldiers he requires. All
those who arrive after this cannot be accepted
and go back home to take their hunting weapons,
leaving directions where they are going to hunt
so that they can be found in case of need. These
late comers receive scant welcome on their return
to their families, who upbraid them for their
lack of zeal in coming to the defense of their
country.[26]

For three days the warriors inside the quadrangle take a war medicine of which I shall
speak later. Their wives bring their arms and the
equipment necessary for the campaign. They
place everything one hundred paces in front of
the square, along with a little bag of Indian corn
or maize, an ounce of which suffices to make a
pint of porridge.[27] It is only necessary to add
some cold water, and in five or six minutes it is

[26]Adair described in some detail the preparations for
war (*History of the American Indians*, 167 ff.).

[27]According to Swan "the complete equipment of a war-
party is simply to each man a gun and ammunition, a
knife, a small bag of gritz, or pounded corn, and two or
three horse-ropes or halters" ("State of the Creek Nation," 280).

as thick as porridge cooked over a fire. Two ounces is sufficient to nourish a man for twenty-four hours. The savages only make use of this porridge when they are at close quarters with the enemy, because then they cannot go hunting.

When the three days of war medicine are over, the chief sets off with his warriors for the general rendezvous appointed by the Grand Chief. Independently of this general medicine, each band chief has a special kind, or rather a talisman, which he religiously carries with him. This is a little bag containing some pebbles and a few scraps of the garment worn by the Grand Chief when he returned from the war. If the band chief should forget this bag, he could not command and would become a common soldier for the duration of the expedition.[28]

The Tastanegy, or Grand War Chief appears at the rendezvous punctually on the day appointed, and he is sure to find the young warriors congregated there. He then places himself at the head of the army and issues the orders that he deems expedient without having to render account for them to anyone. Certain that the discipline and his directives will be promptly

[28]For more about the war-bundle or ark see p. 220. Compare Adair, *History of the American Indians*, 169–171.

carried out, he marches confidently against the enemy.

When the army is thus ready to march, each subordinate chief must be provided with a drink known as war medicine. This is a lightly purgative liquid, which each warrior has to take for three consecutive days before marching off to war.

WAR MEDICINE

The Indians attach very great virtue to this war medicine, and they have such faith in it that it would be difficult for a Grand War Chief to turn his army to account if the warriors were deprived of it.[29] He would be exposed to the greatest danger if, taken by surprise, he were forced to fight before having satisfied this duty. If he suffered a reverse, which could not fail to happen because the soldier would have no confidence and would be defeated in advance by his

---

[29] "Among the Indians the use of war medicine is a religious custom."—Milford. According to Adair the war medicine was "warm water highly imbittered with button-rattle-snake-root" (*History of the American Indians*, 168). Swan spoke of it as "a strong decoction of button snake-root, or senneca, which they use in such quantities as often to injure their health by producing spasms, &c" ("State of the Creek Nation," 268). Swanton identifies this as *Eryngium yuccaefolium* ("Religious Beliefs and Medical Practices of the Creek Indians," 655–656). Other writers do not distinguish between a "big" and a "little" medicine.

superstitious fear, the chief would be accused of having brought on the disaster by his negligence in failing to give out the war medicine, and he would be held responsible for all the events resulting from it.

If this usage is fraught with danger for the chief of the army, it nevertheless provides him in exchange with exceptional means for ensuring the success of his enterprise. There are two medicines, the "big" and the "little," and it is for the Grand Chief to designate which is to be taken. The big medicine fanaticizes the soldier, so to speak. When he has partaken of this, he thinks he is invulnerable, like Achilles dipped in the Styx. The little medicine serves to diminish, in his eyes, the dangers. Full of confidence in his chieftain, he is easily persuaded that, if the little war medicine only is administered, it is because the circumstances do not warrant the big. It therefore rests with the sagacity of the chief to turn this superstition to account.

This medicine, whose moral effect I have just described, has two purely physical effects. The first is that, since the Indians are very fond of strong drink, a way must be found to deprive them of it without causing them to murmur. The medicine, whether big or little, offers such a means, because they are not allowed to drink any liquor before taking it, a regulation that they observe very punctiliously. And the chief, being at liberty to order it whenever he deems expedient, may in this way maintain the utmost sobriety in the army. The second effect is that this medicine is really aperient, and the warrior thus purged finds himself less exposed to danger from his wounds, which, in point of fact, heal very quickly if they are not mortal. These tribes have still another way of reducing the danger from their wounds, and this is by fighting almost naked. They have noted that a woolen garment, of which some particles almost always remain in the wound, makes the latter much more difficult to heal and more dangerous. Thus, policy and religion, one supporting the other, come to each other's aid and turn to the profit of those who know how to employ them expediently.

During a war, the Muskogees observe a very rigorous discipline; they may neither eat nor drink without the permission of their chiefs. I have seen them refrain from drinking even when swimming across a river because circumstances had obliged the chief to prohibit it under penalty of depriving them of their little war medicine, that is to say, of the influence of the talisman.[30]

These people, though endowed with a very martial spirit, live peaceably and do not harrass

[30] "I have already said that the big, or general, medicine is taken before they leave for war."—Milford.

their neighbors; but should an enemy force them to assemble and take up arms, they do not return home till they have fought them and taken their scalps; these might be compared to the flags among European troops. When a Muskogee kills his enemy, he takes the entire scalp, a highly honored trophy on his return to the nation. You would be surprised at the dexterity and swiftness with which they lift the scalp from a man whom they have killed. These scalps are not all of equal merit; they are classified, and it is for the chiefs who have witnessed the exploits to place a value on them. Advancement, both civil and military, is based upon the number and value of these scalps. I am now going to give the reader an idea of the importance the Creeks attach to the scalps of their enemies.

The greater part of the savage tribes of North America rarely take captives in time of war. If by chance they do, then on their return they either burn them alive or torture them to death. For the victim as well as for his executioners it is a feast day; the latter rejoice over the destruction of an enemy of their country, the former that he may die for his. As it is a great honor for a warrior to kill many of his country's enemies, each claimed to have killed the largest number. It became necessary to require some proof before deciding who had done most for his fatherland. This led to the custom of scalping the fallen enemy in order to prove that one had killed him. When I arrived among the Creek's, eligibility for any kind of office was contingent upon having scalped at least seven enemies. A young Creek who had been to war and had not brought back at least one scalp always bore his mother's name and was unable to find a wife. In this nation the children all belong to the mother,[31] who for the first month after her confinement holds the power of life and death over her new-born child. After this time, should she kill it, she herself would be punished with death.

When a young warrior brings in his first scalp, the chief and the warriors of the town where he lives congregate in the Grand Cabin to give him a name and have him drop that of his mother. It is usually the chiefs who estimate the value of a scalp, basing its worth on the dangers one has run in taking it, and the scalps, as I have said before, are the qualifications for advancement and esteem.[32]

---

[31]Descent among the Creeks was matrilineal.

[32]"Young men remain in a kind of disgrace, and are obliged to light pipes, bring wood, and help cook black-drink for the warriors, and perform all the menial services of the public square, until they shall have performed some warlike exploit that may procure them a war-name, and a seat in the square at the black-drink. This stimulates them to push abroad, and at all hazards to obtain a scalp, or as

During the battle, the Grand Chief is usually stationed in the center of the army. He distributes the reserves wherever he thinks the danger greatest, and when he sees that his army is giving way and he fears lest it surrender to the enemy, he then advances in person and fights hand to hand. A war whoop repeated to the right and the left notifies all the warriors of the danger to which their chief is exposed. Immediately all the reserve corps close ranks and march to the place where the Grand Chief is in order to compel the enemy to relinquish him; if he is dead, they would rather all be killed than abandon his body to the foe without first taking his scalp. They attach such dishonor to the loss of this scalp that, when the danger is great and they cannot, despite all their efforts, prevent his falling into the enemy's hands, the warrior nearest the chief kills him himself, takes his scalp, and, running off with a yell known only to the savages, proceeds to the place to which this same chief had directed them to retreat in the event of defeat. All the subordinate chiefs, informed of the

they term it, *bring in hair.* . . . Those who have seldom been abroad, and are not distinguished by war-names, are styled old women, which is the greatest term of reproach that can be used to them" (Swan, "State of the Creek Nation," 280). Swan's description of the reception of a successful young warrior has already been quoted in note 21, p. 25.

death of the Grand Chief by this yell, prepare to retreat, and as soon as that is accomplished and before taking any other measure, they proceed to appoint the new Grand War Chief so that the enemy will not be aware that the first one has been killed.

The Muskogees are very warlike and are not discouraged by defeat; the day after an unsuccessful battle, they march against their enemy as intrepidly as before. Their decision to continue their march to the northwest was inspired by this trait in their character. After marching some time in this direction and after traversing vast plains, they halted in a little wood on the banks of the Missouri River.[33] Here they came up with the Alibamus whom they had been pursuing for a long time. They made suitable preparations to wage war against them. The Tastanegy, or Grand War Chief, directed the march in the following order: the family of the Wind,[34] to which he belonged, crossed the river first; it was followed by the family of the Bear, then by that of the Tiger, and so on. Since the entire nation was on the

[33]An error for Red River?

[34]"It is necessary to point out here that there are certain families in the nation that are held in higher esteem than the others, either because they have shown greater courage or because they have rendered greater services to the country. These same families—that is to say, the young warriors belonging to them—ordinarily lead the

march, it was necessary, after they had passed the river, to take measures to prevent their being surprised by the enemy and, in case of an encounter, to protect all those who could not fight. To this end the young men with their war chiefs formed the vanguard, the old men the rear guard, those of middle age the flanks, with the women and children in the center. They marched in this formation till they caught up with the enemy. Then only the young warriors led by their Tastanegy advanced, leaving the main portion of the nation in a place of safety under the protection of the elders. By a stealthy, well-planned march, they surprised the Alibamus and were upon them in the caverns where they lived before they had any warning. Since the Muskogees gave them no time to rally, the slaughter was very great.

They were so terrified on being caught so unprepared that they abandoned their habitations, fled to the Missouri, and rallied on the banks of this river. Meanwhile the Muskogees went to fetch their compatriots, whereupon they set off again in pursuit of the enemy. The Alibamus, fearing another surprise attack, had sent on in

marching columns and the war chief takes care to preserve this prerogative in so far as circumstances do not necessitate another disposition. It is a source of emulation from which he sometimes derives great advantage."—Milford. Part of McGillivray's ascendancy may be traced to his belonging to the Wind clan.

advance the old men, women, and children whilst the young warriors brought up the rear. They continued for some time to descend the right bank of this river. The Muskogees, following their trail, caught up with them and had several encounters with them. The Alibamus, as soon as they discovered that the enemy was in pursuit, had the main body of the nation cross over to the left bank of the Missouri and then gave them time to get away by skirmishing with the enemy, so as to retard the latter's progress. However, fearing lest they could not hold out against them, they took advantage of a black night to rejoin their fathers without the Muskogees noting it. The latter, finding when day came no signs of the enemy and surmising the direction they had taken, crossed the river and renewed their pursuit. After several days' march they fell in with the Alibamus and compelled them to give battle, in which the latter were put to rout and fled to the banks of the Mississippi. The Muskogees, pursuing them relentlessly, drove them headlong into the river where a very great many perished. The young Muskogee warriors, having thus considerably weakened their foe, gave up the chase till the rest of the nation, which was following by short stages, had caught up with them. They stopped a week on the banks of this river to rest.

Meanwhile, the Alibamus had marched a long distance and were now far in advance. The Muskogees, in trying to overtake them, penetrated deeply into an immense forest on the left bank of the Mississippi, where they encamped; but since there was no advantage in their settling there, the elders resolved to push on farther and for that purpose to send the young warriors to reconnoitre the enemy's position. They marched for several days without coming up with them, but, at length discovering their tracks, they returned to report to the council of elders, who resolved to go in pursuit. They therefore set out once more and, after marching for several days, arrived at the Ohio River, called by the French *La Belle Rivière*.

They followed its banks up to the Wabash and, noting that the Alibamus had crossed the Ohio, they also crossed it. Arriving on the other side and finding a tolerably good climate and a region abounding in every kind of game, they decided to settle there and established their colony in what is known as the Yazoo Country. As the season was well advanced, they gave up their pursuit, merely despatching some young scouts to discover, if they could, the route taken by the Alibamus. The Muskogees, availing themselves of some caves they found and of some others that they made, took possession of the Yazoo lands, where they passed several years and where the caves they excavated may still be seen.[35]

The Alibamus had advanced as far as Coosa River. Seeing that the enemy was no longer in pursuit and finding themselves in a fertile country, they settled there; but in constant fear of a surprise, they sent young warriors out to see what had become of the Muskogees and whether they were still pursuing them. Although the war that the Muskogees then waged against the Alibamus was occasioned by an aggression on the part of the latter, who had killed some Muskogee warriors, the young Alibamus sent out to find them were still imprudent enough to kill the first Muskogees they encountered. The elders, upon learning of this new offense, ordered the Muskogee warriors to march against the Alibamus. Upon discovering that the country inhabited by their enemy was located in the east in a region where the winters were not very severe and where there was a great abundance of game of every kind, the Muskogee warriors resolved for the third time to drive them off and settle in this territory, which was located between the two Floridas.[36] With this intent they crossed the Cumberland and Tennes-

[35]Apparently the author here locates the Yazoo country in Kentucky.

[36]The two Floridas properly speaking were south of the 31st parallel, although West Florida claimed 32° 30″ as its

see Rivers and went north [*sic*] along the banks
of Coosa River, where the remnants of the Alibamus had settled. The latter, hearing that the
Muskogees were on the march, did not deem it
expedient to wait for them. They evacuated their
settlement and dispersed, some seeking refuge
with the Choctaws, others going to Mobile under
the protection of the French, who just then had
taken possession of it.[37]

The Muskogees, finding no more enemies to
fight, calmly took possession of the land they had
just conquered. They settled on the Coosa, Tallapoosa, Chattahoochee, Flint, Ocmulgee, Big and
Little Oconee, and Ogeechee Rivers down as far
as the Savannah in Georgia where the town of
Augusta is now built.

After appropriating this immense domain and
establishing their settlements, they sent young
warriors in pursuit of the Alibamus as far as
Mobile; but since the latter had placed themselves
under the protection of the French, the French
commandant appealed to the chief of the Musko-

---

northern boundary. Milford, however, may have been
thinking of the disputed country east of the Mississippi as
far north as modern Memphis.

[37]Fort Biloxi, or Maurepas, was established in 1699,
Mobile in 1701. Fort Toulouse, among the people Bossu
called the Allibamons, was built in 1714 at the confluence
of the Coosa and the Tallapoosa Rivers. From this junction the stream is called the Alabama.

gee warriors for peace on behalf of the Alibamus. The Muskogee war chiefs, not wishing to take upon themselves the responsibility of making a treaty without the consent of their nation, referred the decision to the council of elders and, while awaiting that decision, agreed to a suspension of hostilities, promising not to kill any Alibamus before receiving a reply from their council, to which they even promised to recommend their enemies on the express condition that the Alibamus in turn would equally respect the Muskogees and avoid as far as possible those hunting grounds where they must pass the winter, each being assigned a distinct range. This truce lasted six months, at the end of which time the elders of the Muskogees came down to Mobile with their warriors and not only made peace between the two nations in the presence of the French commandant but even invited the Alibamus to unite with them; and as an inducement they allocated to them land on the Mobile River, which is still known as the River of the Alibamus. The latter accepted the proposal on the understanding that they be permitted to retain their national manners and usages. Then all the scattered bands united and settled on the river named after them and built a little town which is called Koasati.[38]

[38]No doubt much of what follows Milford learned from McGillivray. Adair was "assured by a gentleman of char-

Since then they have formed an integral part of
the Muskogee nation, which at that time took the
name of the Creek nation. This word means the
source of a river and derives from the nature of
the country where they lived, which, as we have
seen above, is surrounded or intersected by a large
number of good-sized rivers.

Around the same time, an Indian tribe that had
just been destroyed by the Iroquois and Hurons
came to implore the protection of the Muskogees,
which from now on I shall call the Creeks. The
Creeks took them in and assigned them land in
the center of the nation. They built a town called
Tukabahchee, after the name of the Indian tribe,
which is now quite a sizable place. The grand
assemblies of the Creek nation, of which it is a
component part, were sometimes held within its
walls. The warlike reputation of the Creeks, the
friendly welcome they had extended to the Alibamus and the Indian tribe of which I have just
spoken spread rapidly among the other Indian

acter, who traded a long time near the late Alebahma
garrison, that within six miles of it, live the remains of
seven Indian nations, who usually conversed with each
other in their own different dialects, though they understood the Muskohge language; but being naturalized, they
were bound to observe the laws and customs of the main
original body" (*History of the American Indians*, 285). For
a good, brief statement of the complexity of the Creek confederacy see Hodge, *Handbook of North American Indians*,
I, 961–962.

tribes of North America, and those that were too weak to repel the attacks of an enemy soon came to implore their aid. The Taskigis and the Okchas, who had suffered the same treatment from their neighbors as the Tukabahchees, upon learning of the latter's kind treatment by the Creeks, also sought refuge and protection from them. They too were admitted to form part of the nation, were given land to cultivate, and established themselves at the confluence of the Coosa and Tallapoosa Rivers where they built a village still known as Taskigi. The Okchas went ten leagues farther north and settled in a beautiful plain on the banks of a little river where they also built a town to which they gave their name.

A short time later, the remnants of the little Yuchi nation, which had been partially destroyed by the English, also took refuge with the Creeks, who assigned them land on the banks of the Chattahoochee River.[39] A part of the Chickasaw nation likewise sought refuge with the Creeks, who gave them land on the Yazoo River at the head of Wolf

[39]The Koasatis, according to Swanton, were related to but not identical with the Alibamus; their village at this time was a few miles below the junction of the Coosa and the Tallapoosa. The Taskigis (Tuskegees) had come from north of the Tennessee; their town was on the Coosa, a little north of the junction. The Tukabahchee town was the chief and most populous village of the Upper Creeks; it was on the Tallapoosa just below the En-fau-be. The

River. Here they established their settlements, which extended as far as the Cherokee mountains,[40] back of which flows the Tennessee River, which rises in these mountains near Tugaloo on the outskirts of South Carolina, a short distance from the source of the Savannah River in Georgia.

The immense stretch of territory seized by the Muskogees, now the Creeks, after the flight of the Alibamus, made it possible for them to take in all the tribes that demanded this favor of them and to assign them land for tillage. This enhanced their reputation and their ability to sustain it.

Although these tribes so received by the Creeks were incorporated in the nation, it sometimes happened, nevertheless, that they had hostile expeditions of their own. In case of defeat, however, they had the right to appeal for assistance to the Creeks, who aided them either by their arms or their mediation, as will be seen from the following.

Some years after the Chickasaws had joined the Creeks, the unfortunate Natchez nation, which had been almost entirely destroyed by the French,

---

Yuchis had earlier been located on the Savannah River; their town was on the Chattahoochee at the mouth of present Big Uchee Creek. The Okchais were living partly near the old Alabama Fort and partly on Kialaga Creek, a bit above the Tukabahchee town. All these villages are described in Hawkin's *Sketch;* much more about them may be found in Swanton, *Early History of the Creek Indians.*

[40]Cumberland Mountains.

who then possessed Louisiana, found refuge with
these same Chickasaws, who espoused their cause
and marched with them against the French army,
which they met on a little plain near Wolf River.
Here a battle took place in which the French, despite the superiority of their artillery, were completely routed. The savages fell upon them with
such fury that they were hewn to pieces, except
for a mere handful of fugitives who escaped to
tell the tale.[41] The French organized a new army
to continue the war against the Chickasaws, but
the latter, fearing lest they should not be so fortunate a second time, made peace proposals which
the French accepted all the more readily because
they had by no means forgotten the loss inflicted
on them by this people and the courage they had
shown in the Battle of Wolf River. But they continued to pursue the unfortunate remnants of the
Natchez nation, which having constantly to flee
its pursuers, sought a new homeland amongst the
Creeks, who had been recommended to them by
the Chickasaws, also under their protection. They
even represented to the Creeks that, having taken
sides with them against the French, they were

[41]Fort Rosalie was destroyed by the Natchez in November, 1729. The following year the tribe was cut to
pieces by the French and the remnant joined the Chickasaws. Milford probably refers to the defeat of Diron
d'Artaguiette in 1736 by the Chickasaws at Prudhomme
Bluffs in the neighborhood of modern Memphis.

interested parties and almost in duty bound to accord them their support. The Creeks took them in and allocated them land on the Coosa River at the foot of two mountains remarkable alike for their height and their sugar-loaf form, and which from then on were called Natchez. The Natchez built two towns there, to one of which they gave their own name and to the other that of Abihka.[42]

Whilst this nation was establishing its settlements and building towns, the chiefs of the Creeks, their protectors, had gone down to Mobile and New Orleans to negotiate peace with the French. The latter, aware of their military strength and fearing lest a rejection should draw down upon them that warlike nation, as had happened earlier with the Chickasaws, accepted their proposal. They even insinuated to the Creeks that they were flattered at being afforded this opportunity of proving to them that they wished to live in peace with them. Shortly after this the Creeks in turn had occasion to give proof of their personal affection for France by permitting the French to build a fort near the village of Taskigi at the confluence of the two rivers just below this village. The Creeks, the Alibamus, and the Tas-

[42]The Abihkas were an ancient division of the Muskogees who adopted some of the Natchez refugees. Their village was a little east of the Coosa about fifty or more miles north of the junction. The Natchez village was nearby.

kigis then all turned to and helped the French so that they could build it quickly.[43]

The English, who were alarmed by this fort, also requested permission to build one on the Ogeechee River, twenty leagues to the west of Augusta in the backwoods of Georgia. But sanction was refused. They asked the reason why. The Creeks replied in these terms: "The French are the first Europeans with whom we had ties of friendship; we regard them as our fathers and our protectors because they have never abused our confidence or imposed on their friendly intercourse with our nation. You English, on the contrary, whilst giving us a great many presents, exact daily new land grants from us in return so that these presents are very dear-bought. When the French give us a present, it is like a father giving something to his children; they demand no recompense. Hence, they can build all the forts they like, and we shall be content because we look upon them as a protection for ourselves. As for you, we beg you to say nothing further to us on the subject. You are already too close to us. You are like the fires we kindle every year in our forests to destroy the dead underbrush. If we were

[43]Fort Toulouse aux Alibamons (sometimes called Fort Alabama). This had been built fifteen years before the dispersal of the Natchez and two decades before the Chickasaw War.

not there to check their progress, they would soon destroy everything. You too would invade a large part of our domain, or else force us to cede it to you outright. We advise you to be content with what we have given you and to exact nothing more." Such a reply impressed the English and caused them to limit their demands lest they incur the hostility of the Creeks, who under French protection could easily have driven the English from all their possessions in this part of the continent.

Some years after the construction of Fort Toulouse, war broke out between France and England.[44] The French, having lost Canada and being unable to proceed with their projects of colonial expansion, and of which I shall speak in another work, ceded Louisiana to Spain and from then on had no further intercourse with any of the tribes of which I have spoken up till now. When they evacuated Fort Toulouse, they left there four guns, after first destroying the orillions. They are still on the site of the fort.[45]

The Indians were very sad at being thus abandoned by the French since they thereby lost a valuable support and, having no desire to ally themselves with the English or the Spanish, found themselves reduced to their own forces.

[44]That is, four decades later.
[45]Fort Toulouse was evacuated in 1763. Hawkins (*Sketch,* 37–38) and others of his day mention the cannon.

During their alliance with the French, they had learned to use firearms, linen, and other objects employed by the Europeans, with which the French supplied them at that time. The absence of these things proved a very bitter deprivation for them, and they saw themselves obliged to resort to the English in order to obtain them. They established a barter commerce with them, trading peltry for European commodities. From this time on the English have been in full control of this fine branch of commerce. One circumstance that I am going to relate herewith helped at this time to consolidate the authority and credit that the English had acquired over the minds of the Creeks. This is what happened.

At the headwaters of the little river St. Mark of Apalache, the Spanish had three forts, several villages, and beautiful plantations. The priests who were with them undertook to convert to the Christian religion the little Apalachicola and Florida nations and to achieve this end commenced with a gentle and persuasive instruction which won the confidence of the Indian women. They baptised them and then required them to go to confession. It was their intention to change radically the extremely simple customs of these tribes and to have them adopt the usages of civilized society. To this end they represented to these women that certain actions were criminal, actions that hitherto had seemed to them the most natural in the world. They tried to make them less obliging to their husbands; in a word, they gave them advice that by no means furthered domestic peace. The husbands no longer found their wives in such a complying mood as was hitherto their wont. A spirit of discord and bickering had taken the place of the docility and good nature that had formerly ensured domestic peace and happiness. Instead of the virtue that is the ornament of their sex, the young girls exhibited a dissimulation and a duplicity previously unknown.

The Indians being unable to attribute such an unexpected change in the dispositions of their wives and daughters to anything but their acquaintance with the Spanish priests and the counsels of the latter resolved to revenge themselves by prohibiting these priests to enter their houses and forbidding their wives to receive any of them. The priests, seeing that their enterprise was doomed to failure unless they bent all their efforts to effect it, had recourse to the inquisition, invoking all the authority of that frightful tribunal and staining once more with blood the altars of the God of Peace. Each day the unfortunate Indians saw new pyres arise and a large number of their brothers made victims of the blind fury of these fanatics. The Floridians, justifiably appalled at the sight of such a heart-rending spectacle, rose up in mass to throw off such a yoke, but they could not hold out against the Spanish arms and saw violent means employed against them, spreading death and devastation all around. They therefore resolved to appeal to the Creeks for aid against their executioners. The Creeks, who did not like the Spanish, sent warriors to the Floridians, who went down to Apalache and attacked the Spanish troops, who, despite the superiority of their arms, were beaten and forced to abandon their forts and guns. Before leaving, however, they took care to mine the three forts, with the result that the Indians, rashly defying danger, advanced without taking due precaution and thus lost many of their warriors through the explosion of the mines. Incensed by this occurrence and wishing to avenge the death of their brothers, the savages fell on the unfortunate Spanish inhabitants, who no longer having the assistance of the army, which was beating a retreat, were almost all massacred. The Spanish army had time to retire in orderly ranks to Fort St. Mark of Apalache, which was built on foul, marshy ground so that they found only brackish water for their use. Being unable to hold such a position, they took advantage of several dark nights to evacuate the fort, leaving behind their artillery and taking refuge in two little islands situated two leagues farther south that form a bay into which the Apalachicola and Flint Rivers discharge their waters. Shortly after this, Spanish ships arriving from Havana took the rest of the army on board. Since then Fort St. Mark has been abandoned.[46]

The Creeks called these Florida and Apalachicola Indians "Seminoles," meaning foreigners. After the war against the Spanish, of which I have just spoken, these Seminoles, filled with gratitude for the aid rendered them by the Creeks, asked to join the Creek Confederacy and form a component of it. This request, communicated to the council of elders, was granted, and it was decided that in future this tribe should be known as Seminole-Creeks, that they would be incorporated in the confederacy, and that their interests

---

[46] "As I mentioned in Part I, about fifteen years ago the Spanish, with the sanction of the Creek nation, took possession of it again."—Milford. It is hard to say what Milford is talking about in these pages. The Apalachee, who had a number of towns (with Franciscan missions) reaching from Apalachee Bay to Pensacola, were almost wiped out in 1703–04 by a combined attack of Creeks and Carolinian whites. Some remnant were eventually merged with the Creeks (Swanton, *Early History of the Creek Indians,* 119–129). The Apalachiocolas were first settled on the Savannah and later near the junction of the Chattahoochee and the Flint. St. Marks had been occupied by the British in 1766 and abandoned by them two years later. A Spanish detachment under Luis de Bertucat took possession in July 1787 (Boyd, "The Fortifications of San Marcos de Apalache"; Caughey, *McGillivray of the Creeks,* 155, 158).

would be the same. From this time, they adopted, in part, the habits and language of the Creeks. But they lack their frankness and integrity; on the contrary, they have a very great penchant for stealing and pillaging, a trait that always distinguishes them from the Creeks, who have little regard for them and for this reason have kept for them the name of Seminoles.[47] These were the events that destroyed Spanish commerce in this part of the New World and thereby gave to English commerce a firm consistence, which they have known how to maintain.

A short time after the American Revolution, that part of the Shawnee nation inhabiting the upper Savannah River, which was named after this nation, moved north to the banks of the Ohio near Kentucky; the rest joined the Creeks, who ceded them land on the Tallapoosa River near the Alibamus. This nation settled there where it built a little town and follows its own usages and customs. These differ greatly from those of the Creeks, but this does not prevent their getting along perfectly together. They have

[47]The Seminoles were neither Apalachee nor Apalachicola Indians but a separate tribe that moved into the area left vacant by the dispersal of the Apalachees, according to Swanton, *Early History of the Creek Indians*, 398–414. The name, he says, was applied by the Creeks to "people who remove from populous towns and live by themselves."

the same interests, go hunting together on the same hunting range, and in time of war their warriors march side by side and obey the orders of the same Grand Chief. Nevertheless, when a Shawnee marries with a Creek woman, he must adopt the laws, customs, and usages of the latter, which is not the case when a Creek marries with a Shawnee.[48]

The Creek nation, being thus tremendously augmented through the formidable emigrations of numerous contiguous nations, has acquired a consistence that today makes it very powerful and capable of mustering a very large and war-like army. Being the most powerful on the continent, it is the nation that every year, in the grand council of the elders, dictates the national policy for the ensuing year, not only for the constituent nations, of which I have spoken, but even for the savage tribes of almost all North America.

These assemblies, which I attended for twenty years, are usually held the end of April or the beginning of May, as I have already stated. Here they present their complaints or their demands

[48]The dates are wrong. By 1730 the Shawnees of the Savannah River, settled there as early as 1670, had removed to the Chattahoochee, to Florida, to Pennsylvania, and to the Ohio, where the main branch of the tribe had long lived. A French census of 1760 showed a Shawnee village near Fort Toulouse (Swanton, *Early History of the Creek Indians*, 317–320).

of whatsoever nature; here they discuss and order the interests of the entire nation and its confederated tribes. Assemblies are sometimes held in the month of September before leaving for the hunt, but these are not general assemblies; few matters of importance are handled, and strangers are rarely present.

The Cherokees who inhabit the Cumberland and Kentucky mountains have also been driven, under English and American pressure, to take refuge on Creek territory and have become their loyal allies. The only nation in that immense stretch of territory whose interests and customs are absolutely foreign to the Creeks is the Choctaw. This nation, which inhabits the territory west of the Alibamus and was formerly very powerful, can still easily muster an army of six thousand warriors.

THE CHICKASAWS ABANDON THE CUSTOM OF BURYING ALIVE THE WIFE OF A WARRIOR WHEN HE DIES

As for the Chickasaws, of whom I have already spoken and who live on the banks of the Yazoo River, they are now so reduced in number that they could scarcely muster six hundred men. About forty years ago, this nation still had the horrible custom, when a warrior died, of burying his wife alive with him. They were both placed in a sort of pit into which were thrown all the warrior's weapons and all his household utensils. To this were added some victuals, and then the pit was filled up and the woman suffocated, in order, so they said, nevermore to leave her husband, and to accompany him on his way.

As this nation forms part of the Creek nation and sends its chiefs to the general assemblies, the Creeks succeeded in making these chiefs see the dreadful barbarity of such a custom and in persuading them to induce the Chickasaw nation to abandon it. On this occasion the grand council even brought all its authority to bear and threatened not to admit these chiefs to any more assemblies and to break off all relations with the Chickasaws and take away their lands if they retained this horrible custom. The latter, fearing the effects of such a menace, abandoned this frightful custom and became good fathers and good husbands, and yet have conserved an intrepidity that is peculiarly their own.[49]

[49]Was Milford confusing this with the ancient custom of the Natchez to sacrifice the widows of the Suns? Among the Chickasaws there seems no foundation for his account. Adair said that the Chickasaw widow was expected to mourn for three years, leading a "chaste single life . . . [refraining from] all public company and diversions, at the penalty of an adultress." However, "if she be known to lament her loss with a sincere heart, for the space of a year, and her circumstances of living are so strait as to need a change of her station—and the elder brother of her deceased husband lies with her, she is thereby exempted

These are the nations, or rather the remnants of nations, that have contributed to the aggrandizement and the high reputation of the Creeks today.

I have just said that the Choctaw nation is the only one whose customs and interests differ from the Creeks. I am now going to give an idea of their usages and character.

DISGUSTING USAGES AND CUSTOMS
OF THE CHOCTAWS

The Choctaw nation is still quite large; it is divided into two parts or colonies, one of which is in the south and the other in the north. The customs and character of the inhabitants of these two provinces are so diametrically different that they might be taken for two distinct tribes, though they are absolutely one and the same nation and speak the selfsame language.[50]

from the law of mourning. . . . The warm-constitutioned young widows keep their eye so intent on this mild beneficent law, that they frequently treat their elder brothers-in-law with spirituous liquors till they intoxicate them, and thereby decoy them to make free, and so put themselves out of reach of that mortifying law. If they are disappointed, as it sometimes happens, they fall on the men, calling them *Hoobuk Wakse*, or *Skoobále, Hassé kroopha*, 'Eunuchus praeputio detecto, et pene brevi;' the most degrading of epithets" (*History of the American Indians*, 195–199).

[50]For the divisions of the Choctaws see Swanton, *Choctaw Social and Ceremonial Life*, 55 ff.

The Choctaws of the north are very brave and warlike; they wear clothes and crop their hair like the Creeks.

The Choctaws of the south, who live west of Mobile and northwest of Pascagoula, are not very warlike; they are cowardly, lazy, and filthy. Although their land is quite fertile, they neglect to cultivate it and prefer a life of mendicancy. Several times a year they go down to Mobile and New Orleans to beg. When they arrive, the Governor gives them food gratis for three days and does not allow them to stay any longer. This gift of food, though voluntary on the part of the Spanish Governor, has degenerated into a habit that they look upon as obligatory, and, if the Governor refuses it, they engage in plundering and all kinds of excesses. At the end of the three days, they prepare to leave and are again given food for a week, ample time to return to their own territory, though they take much longer. They usually leave at once and go back by way of Lake Pontchartrain, though they often stop in Bay St. Louis and Pascagoula where they beg from the inhabitants, who give them Indian corn. This serves them for porridge, sagamity, and bread, which they eat with the fish they catch in Mobile Bay and the rivers in the vicinage, all of them full of fish. They are exceedingly fond of horse flesh, and, when they find any dead horses, even those that have died a natural death, they prefer it to beef or any other meat. These savages are so lazy and so filthy that they never cleanse any part of the body. As they go practically naked, their bodies are caked with dirt, which in the course of time becomes the color of soot. The only garment they wear is a loincloth of woolen material or deerskin passed between their legs and the two ends of which, attached to strings, serves them as belt. The women wear a sort of skirt of the same material, which covers them from the waist to the knees. The rest of the body is naked. Some among them who, as wives of good hunters, are richer than the rest wear round their shoulders a white, red, or blue woolen shawl.

They are very fond of wearing little bells like those one fastens to dog collars in Europe. When they can procure any by barter or by purchase, they attach them to a kind of garter made of deerskin, which they wear above the knee. The young bucks with this adornment are very proud of it and think it makes them more attractive to the girls, who, in turn, to prettify themselves pierce the septum of the nose and insert a ring to which is attached a pear-shaped pendant similar to our earrings.

Here it is necessary to observe that all the savages of North America are very fond of this ornament and habitually wear it. I too had to have my nose pierced so that I could wear a pendant like the savages when I marched at their head.

BURIAL CUSTOMS OF THE CHOCTAWS

In traveling in this nation, I witnessed their burial customs, which seemed to me so remarkable that the reader will not mind my giving him some idea of them.

When a Choctaw dies, his relatives erect at a distance of twenty to twenty-five paces directly opposite his door a scaffold on which they deposit the corpse wrapped in a bear or buffalo skin or a woolen blanket and then leave it there for seven or eight months. The nearest women relatives come each morning to wail, walking round and round the scaffold. When they think the body is in a sufficient state of putrefaction for the flesh to be removed easily from the bones, they notify the priest or medicine man of the district where the dead man lived, who is charged with the most disgusting dissection imaginable. As all the relatives and friends of the dead man must be present at this ceremony, which terminates with a family feast, the priest fixes a day that will allow time for everyone to be notified, and on the appointed date they all gather round the scaffold where, after making hideous grimaces in token of their grief, they sing mournful dirges in which they give expression to their sorrow over their recent bereavement. When they have finished this appalling hubbub, the priest mounts the scaffold, removes the bearskin or blanket covering the corpse and, with his fingernails (for he is not permitted to use anything else), scrapes the bones clean of any flesh that may still be adhering to them. When he has finished this revolting operation, he makes one bundle of the flesh, which he leaves on the scaffold to be burnt, and another of the bones, which he carries down on his head and delivers to the relatives of the deceased, making them an appropriate speech. As soon as the relatives receive the bones, they examine them very carefully to be sure that the priest has forgotten none. They then put them in a sort of chest, closing the opening with a board; after which the women light torches of pitch pine, and the nearest relatives march in procession to deposit the chest in a cabin that serves as the family ossuary.

Whilst the priest is busy with the dissection on the scaffold, all those present occupy themselves in turn with kindling fires on which they place huge earthen pots full of viands for the guests. When the food is cooked, they remove it from the fire to let it cool, but without touching it, for only a priest is permitted to remove the

lids and he may do so only when he has completed his task.

When the ceremony of interring the bones is
concluded, a large quantity of dry wood is stacked
round the scaffold on which the flesh has been
left. The relatives set fire to it and, whilst the
scaffold is burning, dance round it, uttering
shrieks of joy; then the priest selects a suitable
place where they all sit down in a circle, he remaining in the center with the pots of food for
the feast, which have been allowed sufficient
time to cool. When each person has taken his
place, the medicine man or priest removes the
lids of the pots and, without even so much as
washing his hands, which he has merely wiped
off with grass, he dips them into the stew and
takes out the meat, dividing it amongst the relatives and friends of the deceased according to
their rank, and then in the same proportion
serves them with soup and sagamity, which is
their beverage.[51]

I have already mentioned that these people
have a special predilection for horse flesh, which
they prefer to every other kind; with the result
that, should the deceased have been rich enough
to own any horses, they sometimes kill as many

[51]Bartram (*Travels,* 514–515) has a similar description.
Swanton discusses these customs in detail in *Choctaw
Social and Ceremonial Life,* 170–194.

as three, which they cook and with whose flesh they do the honors of the feast. It can happen that, if the deceased possessed no horses, those of his relatives who do have some sacrifice them for this ceremony. This reunion of relatives and friends cannot break up till every particle of food has been consumed so that, if they are unable to eat everything at one sitting, they dance or engage in violent exercise in order to work up an appetite so that they can finish what is left. When nothing more remains, each returns to his own home.

This was not the only bizarre ceremony I witnessed. I shall now describe another that seemed to me no less amazing than the first.

The Choctaws have very great respect for the priests or medicine men, of whom I have just spoken, and in whom they have blind confidence, which the latter often abuse. These medicine men charge high for their attentions to an invalid and almost always in advance. They are so avaricious that, when an illness is of long duration and the invalid is no longer in a position to pay the medicine man, the latter calls a meeting of the sick man's family and informs them that he has given their relative every possible care, that he has employed all the resources of his art, but that the disease is incurable and can end only with his life. The family, after this, decide that, since the invalid has already suffered a long time and there is no hope of his recovery, it would be inhuman to prolong his misery and that it is right and just to put an end to it. Thereupon one or two of the strongest among them go to see the invalid, ask him in the presence of his entire family how he feels, and then, whilst he is replying to this question, throw themselves on him and strangle him.[52]

In 1782, one of these savages, who had been ill for a long time and no longer had the wherewithal to pay his medicine man, was in danger of being strangled, as I have just described. As he was afraid of this and was on his guard, he waited till his family had assembled to hear the report of the medicine man and decide to end his sufferings by killing him. He seized this moment to decamp and avoid the ceremony that was in store for him. He dragged himself as best

---

[52]Bernard Romans reported the same thing but without charging the medicine men with avariciousness: "if a disorder is obstinate or incurable, the relations of the patient assemble in his house, bewail his misfortune, cry bitterly, take their leave of him, and he tells them how tired he is of life, that his misfortunes are unsufferable, and that it is good he should die; upon this an universal howl is raised, the nearest male relation jumps on him, and violently in a moment breaks the neck of the patient, and then they rejoice that his misery is over, and the lamentations for his departure soon succeed" (*History of East and West Florida,* 88).

he could to a wood, which fortunately was close to his habitation. He was unable to take with him any kind of food and was reduced to living from the flesh of woodrats, known as opossums, which is very palatable and very healthful. His family was terribly surprised to find him gone, but the medicine man persuaded them that he had slipped away only to conceal his death, which was inevitable.

Whilst this unfortunate savage was thus wandering in the wood, he remembered that he had gone to the Creeks on several occasions to bring them, on behalf of the chiefs of his nation, the strands of beads, or chaplets, that served as records. He resolved to seek refuge with them and to tell them why he had been forced to flee his own country, never doubting that he would find help and protection in such a generous nation. He therefore went to see McGillivray, who was then Grand Chief, and told him the reason for his journey, reminding him that he had been to see him several times on behalf of his chiefs. McGillivray received him courteously, though he did not recognize him since he looked like a skeleton. McGillivray gave him the food of which he was in need and after several days, as he was still ill, had him take an emetic diluted with an infusion of sassafras. This medicine cured his malady, but, as he had suffered greatly and had

been ill for a long time, he stayed with McGillivray four or five months in order to recuperate.
I saw him frequently, and he himself told me of
his experience. When he felt perfectly well again,
he returned to his nation. It was then about
eight months since his flight, and his family had
erected a scaffold and performed all the usual
ceremonies that precede and accompany a burial,
as I have described above. He arrived precisely
on the day of the funeral feast and found his
family assembled and his funeral pile on fire, as
though his corpse were on it. The medicine man
had so firmly convinced this savage's relatives
that he could never recover from his malady that,
when he appeared in their midst, they thought
he was a ghost, and all ran away, leaving him
alone. He then went to one of his neighbors,
who, terrified as the rest, threw himself on the
ground and, taking him for a specter, spoke to
him in this wise: "Why did you leave the abode
of the spirits if you were happy there? Why do
you come back here? Just to be present at the
last feast which your family and friends are giving for you? Be off with you! Go back to the
Country of the Dead, lest you revive the grief
they felt over your death!"

Seeing that he was everywhere an object of
terror, the savage resolved to return to the
Creeks, where later he met several of his rela-

tives, who used to go there every year. Only then did he succeed in disabusing them and convincing them that the medicine man had deceived them. His relatives, furious at such rascality, went to see the medicine man, heaped reproaches upon him, and ended by killing him so that he would deceive no one else. They then did everything they could to persuade this savage to come back to them, but he always refused to do so and married a woman of the Taskigi nation by whom he had three children. He is still living where Fort Toulouse formerly stood. The four dismantled guns left by the French at the time of their retreat, of which I have already written, are just opposite his door.

Before leaving the history of this people, I shall here narrate an incident which I witnessed personally, and which seemed to me so extraordinary that I have no hesitancy in relating it.

THE WAY THE CHOCTAWS DIVORCE
A WOMAN TAKEN IN ADULTERY

When a Choctaw woman is taken in adultery, her husband has the right to put her away, but this repudiation is preceded by an astonishing ceremony. The husband, before he can divorce his wife, first calls together his friends, some of his wife's relations, and as many young men as he can find, without informing her of it. When

they are all assembled, he selects one of the
group and sends him to find out if the woman is
at home. When they learn that she is, they sur-
round the house. The husband goes in with two
of the woman's relations, seizes her and carries
her off to a field where the savages usually play
ball. (The savages are all very fond of this game.)[53]
They stop at the edge of the field and at once
despatch two youths to cut down a sapling,
strip off the bark and fix it in the ground about
a quarter of a league from where the spectators
are. This white post, set up in this way, can be
seen from a great distance. On their return, the
two youths who planted the pole give a signal
whereupon all the witnesses sit down on the
ground with their legs crossed. When they are
all seated, the husband takes his wife by the
hand and leads her about twenty-five paces in
front of the assembly, where he removes her
skirt, leaving her stark naked. He then points to
the pole and says to her: "Run! If you get there
first, you are divorced without other formality;
however, if you're caught, you know the law!"

The woman starts off at once and runs as fast
as she can in order to reach the pole before her
pursuers catch her, for, at her signal to start, the

[53]Bartram described the Choctaw ball game (*Travels*,
506–507). For a full treatment see Swanton, *Choctaw
Social and Ceremonial Life*, 140 ff.

witnesses who, as I have said, are seated on the ground with their legs crossed, jump up and run after her to try to catch her. As the Choctaws are very excellent runners, it is rare indeed for her to reach the goal first.

If she arrives at the white post first, the husband has no further authority over her, and her divorce is pronounced from this fact alone; but should one of the witnesses catch her, she must submit to the carnal desires of all those who demand it of her. Ordinarily the person who catches her is the first to exercise his rights in this respect; then all the others follow suit in turn if they care to do so. It rests entirely with them. Since there is probably no people on earth with more disgusting habits than the Choctaws, the adulterous woman is almost always forced to pay the full penalty and satisfy the brutal lasciviousness of those whom her husband had chosen to dishonor her. When each one has exercised his rights, the husband presents himself to the woman and says: "You are free now, you can join the man with whom you have dishonored me." She is then at liberty to return to her relatives or to remarry without the consent of her family. If she has any children, the girls remain with her and the boys go to their father's family.[54]

[54]"With the Choctaws, as with the Creeks, the children belong to the mother; they are divided only in the case of

One day I happened to witness this extraordinary and shocking ceremony. This is how it came about.

In returning from the caverns of the Red River with my two hundred young warriors, we passed through a Choctaw village, and I had them encamp in a field a short distance from the village while I stopped behind to take some refreshment. I was invited to attend this ceremony, of which I had never heard. I went to the field where it was to take place and there I found a crowd of about thirty men assembled, with one woman in their midst. As soon as I arrived, the man who had invited me took the woman by the hand and led her to a point about twenty-five paces distant, as I have said, and there removed her skirt, the only garment she wore. At this signal she started off with amazing swiftness, but she could not keep up the pace and was caught before she reached the goal. The winner paid me the compliment of offering me his privileges, of which they had told me, but, as I was not anxious to avail myself of them, he exercised his right before the entire assembly, which then followed his lead. Having little curiosity to be

divorce."—Milford. Bossu (*Nouveaux Voyages*, II, 82) and Romans (*History of East and West Florida*, 86–87) confirm Milford on the punishment for adultery, but no other writer makes such a statement about division of the children.

present at such a loathsome spectacle, I returned to the village where a little later I met the woman, who did not seem to me to be very greatly affected by the humiliation to which she had just been subjected.

I left the Choctaw nation to go to Mobile and shortly after went on to Pascagoula and Bay St. Louis, from where I went to New Orleans. In Part I, I have given an account of the things that struck me as most notable in this town and on my journey to the Red River as well as on my return journey from that river to the Creek nation.

I have given an idea of the traits and customs of that nation. I am now going to relate two anecdotes, the first illustrating more particularly its rigorous probity and the bad reputation, even in this nation, of the Seminoles with whom the famous General Bowles has cast his lot; the second, the quick-wittedness of these savages and the dishonesty of the Anglo-Americans.

I witnessed personally the two incidents that I am going to relate.

A SAVAGE'S REMORSE

In 1787, the Spanish took possession again of the fort of the Apalaches and rebuilt it with the sanction of the Creek nation, which McGillivray, their Grand Chief, and I, their Tastanegy, had obtained for them. It was reconditioned by a

Frenchman named Verducas, a captain of engineers in the service of Spain, as I have already said.[55]

McGillivray and I had gone to St. Mark of Apalache to recommend the Spaniards to the chiefs of the Apalaches and the Floridians. When they had taken over the fort, we set out on our return journey, accompanied only by two negroes to look after our horses. We arrived at the banks of the Ochlockonee River, which is always as cold as ice and just then was considerably swollen by the rain that had fallen a few days earlier. There was no way to cross this river but to swim across on our horses, and we were preparing to do so when a savage came up to us and offered to transport us to the other side, saying that the river was too broad and the water too cold for us to reach the opposite bank without danger. As for himself, having to cross it every day, he did not mind the icy water.

It was not without some trepidation that we accepted this man's offer, not knowing how he

[55]See note 46, page 194. McGillivray, 10 July 1887, wrote to O'Neill that he "had sent down to the Lower Towns to have Lieut. Verduca favorably received with his detachment at St. Marks." In November he himself was at that place. In none of the few letters extant for the latter half of 1787 is Milford mentioned, though it is likely that he accompanied McGillivray to St. Marks (Caughey, *McGillivray of the Creeks,* 155, 158, 163–165).

was going to execute it, when we saw him take a cowhide and stretch it over several hoops in the form of a little canoe solid enough to enable us to cross the river without danger. He next took a rope, which he tied to the canoe and wrapped round his body in the form of a shoulder belt; then leaping into the river he brought us, first one and then the other, to the opposite bank.[56] He made eleven trips to carry us and our equipment across and, though each time we made him take a little rum, he was so exhausted that he was unable to ferry our negroes over; so they were obliged to swim across, which so chilled them that one of them died the next day.

This brave Indian's only garment was a worn woolen blanket which, when we were all across, he wrapped round him and went to lie down at the foot of a tree a short distance from us. As night was coming on, we decided to sleep on the bank of this river, and to this end we set up a tent, which McGillivray always carried with him. The savage, noting our intention, remained under his tree to pass the night there. The sky was overcast, and when it began to rain, we sent the Indian word to come and lie down in our tent; he refused to do so despite all our urgings. McGillivray asked him why, after having rendered

[56]Bartram describes such a boat and crossing (*Travels*, 457).

us such a great service, he should now decline our invitation. He replied to us in a manner as edifying as it was amazing.

"You do not know me. I am disgraced and am not worthy of being in the company of virtuous men like you. I come from the town of Kasihta.[57] I was weak enough to steal from one of my neighbors and to keep the stolen object for twelve days, at the end of which time, my senses, which I no doubt had lost, returned to me, and I gave back the object which I had taken. I left immediately with my wife and my three children, and I should have made away with myself if my affection for my family had not been stronger than my despair. It was my idea to settle among the Seminoles; this was the only tribe to which I could go because they are no better than I am, but, fearing to run into some virtuous men there, I preferred to settle quite by myself on the banks of the pond that you saw just before you got to the river. I have a very comfortable house there and I am happy with my family. When I have any peltry I trade it for blankets and other commodities which we need, and I have made up my mind to pass the rest of my life in this way."

Such were the observations of this truly virtuous man, whose obstinacy we were unable to

[57]"Kasihta is near the first town I came to when I arrived in the Creek nation. It is one of the principal towns in the territory."—Milford. Kasihta headed the peace side of the Lower Creek towns; it was on the Chattahoochee a few miles below Coweta, which headed the war side. Hawkins described Kasihta at some length (*Sketch,* 57–59).

overcome. His remorse touched us very deeply, and next day we gave him several little presents in gratitude for the service he had rendered us and left him, thoroughly convinced that he did not merit being banished to the Seminole nation, which is a far more suitable place for Mr. Bowles, who no doubt will not risk showing himself in another part of the nation where he would be certain to meet with the punishment he deserves for the several thefts he has committed.

I have said that the Creeks are quick-witted and intelligent. The following anecdote will prove it, as well as the dishonesty of the Americans.

QUICK-WITTEDNESS OF A CREEK AND THE DISHONESTY OF THE AMERICANS

In 1789, we held, McGillivray and I, on the Oconee River, where the Americans have since built a fort which they call Rock Landing, a conference with the Anglo-Americans for the purpose of discussing terms of peace. There were fifteen hundred Americans under the command of General Twiggs and Clark, the Georgian, as well as a commissioner from Congress and three commissioners from Georgia; and on our side only three hundred men, who were under my command.[58]

[58]The year is correct, even though Milford is *not* mentioned in any of the official correspondence. The abortive

Despite the moderation of McGillivray's proposals, it was impossible to conclude a treaty. One day during the conferences, he gave me some dispatches to deliver to the American commissioners. I took six savages with me, and, on arrival at our destination, one of my men stopped an American and reclaimed his beautiful mount, alleging that the horse had been stolen from him. As the American refused to surrender it, the matter was referred to the American commissioners. The thief insisted that the horse was his, that he had reared it on his plantation, and that he still had the dam. At the same time he asked to be permitted to produce fifty witnesses to the truth of his claims. Since I knew that my savage was an honest man incapable of telling a lie, I begged the commissioners to grant this request. The American went out at once and soon came back with twenty-five of his countrymen who testified that this horse had been reared by their comrade. I then asked these witnesses to swear on the Bible to the truth of their claims, which they did at once. I thereupon apprised my savage (for he did not understand their language)

meeting at Rock Landing in Georgia was held in October, 1789 (see note 100, page 99). McGillivray (writing to Panton, 8 October 1789), however, gave the Creek strength as "nine hundred chosen men" and that of the Commissioners as four hundred (Caughey, *McGillivray of the Creeks*, 254).

of what had taken place and told him that he would have to abandon the horse.

He pondered a moment, then suddenly seizing the blanket that he had around his shoulders, threw it over the horse's head and demanded that the American tell the judges in which eye the horse was blind. The American, taken by surprise, said that his horse was blind in the left eye. My savage declared, on the contrary, that it was not blind in either eye, which fact was immediately substantiated, as well as the dishonesty of the American and his witnesses. The commissioners, no longer doubting the truth, ordered the thief as punishment to return to the savage the horse along with its harness. I informed the latter of the sentence and had the horse turned over to him, but he at once took off the saddle and bridle and threw them at the feet of the American, saying that he would never use anything that had belonged to a thief, that it was no doubt the *Natchoka*[59] which had made them so tricky and wicked.

THE CEREMONY THAT TAKES PLACE ON RETURN
FROM A HOSTILE EXPEDITION

In writing of the war medicine, I said that each band chief must have his own special medi-

[59]"The Indians call books and all printed matter *natchoka*."—Milford.

cine, which consists of a little bag containing some pebbles and scraps of cloth. The origin of the latter is as follows:

When a campaign is over and the army returns, all the band chiefs accompany the Tastanegy, or Grand War Chief, to the door of his house, and there the two eldest war chiefs help him to dismount and then remove all his garments.

Whilst this is taking place, two other chiefs hand him a strip of bark and two leaves of a tree which are to serve as a loincloth. As soon as he is undressed, the two elders who have removed his clothes tear them in tiny pieces and distribute these among all the band chiefs who have taken part in the expedition, and each one places his share in the little medicine bag of which I have spoken.

The army attaches such great virtue to this little bag that, should any chief forget it, he could not command. When the distribution has thus been made, they sing a war song, each fires a shot of his gun, and they then disperse to return to their respective habitations.

I am going to give a brief account of the birth and family of McGillivray and tell how he came to be appointed Beloved Man and Supreme Chief of the savages composing the Creek nation.

HOW MCGILLIVRAY CAME TO BE
APPOINTED BELOVED MAN

Alexander McGillivray was the son of a Creek Indian woman of the Wind clan, the natural daughter of a French officer who formerly commanded Fort Toulouse in the territory of the Alibamus.[60] His father was a Scotchman and had a fur trading business in the Creek nation where he made the acquaintance of McGillivray's mother, whom he married and by whom he had five children, two boys and three girls. As his trading activities brought him into very frequent contact with these savages, he had learned their language perfectly. Of the two sons, only Alexander survived; he lost the second son and two of his daughters.[61] In this country all the children belong to the mother, and McGillivray's father had to obtain his wife's permission to send his

[60]His mother's name was Sehoy; it is said that she was the daughter of a Captain Marchand.

[61]McGillivray had at least two sisters surviving, the elder being Sophia who was married as early as 1783 to a halfbreed named Durand or Durant and had eight children (Caughey, *McGillivray of the Creeks,* 62; Hawkins, *Sketch,* 37, 40). Caughey gives Milford's wife's name as Jeannet. Hawkins (in 1798–99) gave the second sister as "Sehoi. . . . She has one son David Tale, who has been educated in Philadelphia and Scotland." Could there have been three sisters? Milford seems to have been separated from his Creek wife by 1792.

son to Charleston, where he had him given a most excellent education. Alexander did not return to his family till the outbreak of the American Revolution. As his father had gained the friendship of these savages and his mother belonged to the Wind clan, the leading family of the nation, he was received, on the strength of this, in a very considerate and friendly manner by all the chiefs of the nation. In addition, he had come on behalf of the English to invite the chiefs to meet at the frontier for the purpose of making a treaty with them against the Anglo-Americans. At that time the Creeks liked the English because they gave them wonderful presents and numerous negroes. McGillivray, having arrived in the nation under such favorable auspices, the chiefs decided to appoint him their *isti àtagàgi*, Beloved Man. At the time of my arrival this was the only title he had, but he was held in very great esteem. It was when I was made Tastanegy, or Grand War Chief, that he was appointed Supreme Chief. It was only on this condition that I accepted the position offered me by the elders and the chiefs of the nation. I eagerly seized this occasion to prove to McGillivray my deep gratitude for the marks of friendship that he had shown me. We were both invested with our titles in the town of Tukabahchee and from that moment on we were the most intimate of friends, up to the time of his death, which took place at Pensacola, February 17, 1793, at eleven o'clock at night in the house of Panton, our common friend.

HOW I CAME TO MARRY MCGILLIVRAY'S SISTER

I had been about two years among the Creeks without manifesting any desire to marry a woman of this nation, or even to have anything to do with any of them. My long and frequent journeys and the color of this people banished all such ideas from my mind. It was a rather singular adventure that put an end to my celibacy. The reader will surely not mind my relating it.

McGillivray and I had gone to the town of Coweta where he was to hold a grand council. As the opening date had not been set, all the band chiefs had not yet arrived. The inhabitants gave a fete for us while waiting for the council to open. I must state that these fetes last three days, and during this time the women and young girls enjoy unrestricted liberty, especially when they dance the Snake Dance. They then are free to ogle and flirt with the men as much as they like. It was the first such festival I had attended, and I had not been warned of all that might take place. The women of the nation had very quickly noticed my lack of interest in them, and I had reason to believe that they had formed a plan to find out the cause of such indifference. They set one of the prettiest girls in town, young and interesting looking, to entice me. The other women had clubbed together to get her a beautiful printed cotton skirt, a fine chemise, some silver pins, two pairs of bracelets, also of silver, an enormous quantity of many-colored ribbons in her hair, and five pairs of graduated earrings. It was in this gala dress that she presented herself to me and chose me for her cavalier. She struck me as pretty, compared to the rest, and I responded readily to the special attentions she paid me. After spending some time at the festival, we agreed to meet in a more secluded spot as soon as the dances were over. She left very shortly, and I followed her to her mother's house; when we arrived there, she told me that she was going to her room, which was up in the loft. I got ready to betake myself there, but the ladder leading up to it was such a miserable affair that I was a little afraid that it would give way under me. However, I climbed up to the loft and had no sooner arrived than four persons suddenly laid hold of me, which greatly surprised me in a place where I thought I was quite alone. I saw four women who taunted me very gaily with my continence and said that never before had they seen a "capon" warrior (such is the translation of the expression which they used), and that they were

not going to let me go till they were assured of
the contrary. Although I had just finished eating
and my senses were a little excited by the good
cheer and the allurements and amorous glances
of the young girl, it still seemed a fierce assault
to sustain. Yet I had to prove to these women
that a French warrior is as good as a Creek. I
emerged from the combat with honor, and it was
not long before everyone knew of my adventure.

When the council was over, I went back with
McGillivray. He said to me en route: "I always
thought you had an insurmountable aversion to
the women of this nation, just as I found it hard
to get used to them, but your adventure in
Coweta proves the contrary. The friendship that
binds us gives me the right to propose that you
marry my sister. She knows English and the
language of the savages and for this reason could
sometimes be of great service to you and act as
your interpreter."

I was too fond of McGillivray and too grateful
for all he had done for me to refuse an offer
which was renewed proof of his interest in me. I
replied that I was extremely flattered at the
preference shown me and that, if I were as acceptable to his sister as to him, there would be
no objections on my part. A few days after our
return I did, indeed, become his brother-in-
law. This alliance served to gain for me the gen-

eral esteem and confidence of the nation, where I lived very happily for twenty years.

At present I am only awaiting, as I said in Part I of this work, the orders of the French Government to return to these Indians, whose honesty and sincerity are perfectly attuned to my character.

NOTE ON PROPER NAMES

MILFORD spelled by ear. For convenience of reference all proper names in this translation have been given in the now accepted form. In the following list the standard version is followed by the variations in the *Mémoire ou Coup-d'-Oeil*.

Abenaki	Owabenaki
Abihka	Abecouchy
Alibamus	Alibamons
Altamaha	Holtomio
Apalachees	Apalachiens
Apalachicola	Apalachikola
Arkansas	Akancas
Arnold	Arnel
Bergen	Berg
Bowles	Bowls
Caddo	Cado
Carondelet	Carondellet
Chat or Chatot	Chats
Chattahoochie	Chactas-ou-Guy, Chataoudguy, Chattaougy
Chaudpisse	Chaudpine
Cherokees	Cherokys, Cheroquis, Scherokys
Chickasaws	Chikachas, Sikasaos
Choctaws, Lower	Tchactas du Bas
Choctaws, Upper	Tchactas du Haut
Clinton	Clintown
Connecticut	Tucuman

Coosa	Cousa, Coussa
Cornell, Joe	Yocornel
Coweta	Coetas
Crackers	Crakeurs
Creeks	Crëcks
Dunmore	Danemours
Galvez	Galves
Gougers	Gaugeurs
Iberville	Hyberville
Isti àtcagàgi (beloved men)	Estechacko
Jersey	Jarsey
Kasihtas	Cacistas, Kacistas
Kaskaskias (or Cahokias)	Kakias
Kentucky	Quintock, Quintok, Quintokey
Koasati	Coussehaté
Leslie	Laislet
McGillivray	Maguilvray
Miller	Miler
Miro	Mirau, Mireaux
Mississippi	Mississipi
Muskogees	Moskoquies
Natchez	Natches
Natchitoches	Nakitoches
Navarro	Navarre
Newport	Nieuport
New York	New Yorck
Norwich	Noraige, Norege
Oakfuskee	Okfoski
Ochlockonee	Oklocnay, Okylocnay
Ocmulgee	Okmolgy, Okmulgy
Oconee	Aukony, Occony, Oconi, Oconis
Ogeechee	Auguichet, Aukichet, Oguichet

Okchais	Oxiailles
Osages	Ozages
Pascagoula	Paskagola, Paskagoula
Pensacola	Pantsakola, Pantsakole
Rock Landing	Roclandin
Savannah	Savanha
Scioto	Sciotot
Seminoles	Simonolays, Symonolays
Shawnees	Savanhaugay, Savanogues
Swan	Souane, Souanne
Tallapoosa	Talapause
Tallassie	Talessy
Taskigi	Taskiguy, Tasquiguy
Tennessee	Tenessy
Tugaloo	Tougoulou
Tukabahchee	Tuket-bachet
Twiggs	Towigues
Vegas	Viegas
Whigs	Wigth
Yazoo	Yazau
Yorktown	Yorkton
Yuchi	Udgi

SOURCES CONSULTED

MANUSCRIPT

Memoirs and letters submitted by Milford (over the signatures François Tastanegy and General Milford Tastanegy) to the French government and papers relating to him, 1796–1802, in the Archives Nationales, Paris.

PRINTED

Adair, James. *The History of the American Indians.* Edited by Samuel Cole Williams. Watauga Press, Johnson City, Tenn., 1930.

American State Papers, Foreign Affairs. Vol. I.

American State Papers, Indian Affairs. Vol. 1.

Bartram, William. *Travels through North and South Carolina, Georgia, East and West Florida, the Cherokee Country, the Extensive Territories of the Muscogulgees or Creek Confederacy, and the Country of the Chactaws.* 2nd edition, London, 1794.

Bast, Homer. "Creek Indian Affairs, 1775–1778," *Georgia Historical Quarterly,* XXXIII, 1–25 (March, 1949).

(Baynton, Benjamin). *Authentic Memoirs of William Augustus Bowles, Esquire, Ambassador from the United Nations of Creeks and Cherokees to the Court of London.* London, 1791.

Bemis, Samuel Flagg. *Pinckney's Treaty.* Baltimore, 1926.

Berry, Jane M. "The Indian Policy of Spain in the Southwest, 1783–1795," *Mississippi Valley Historical Review,* III, 462–477 (March, 1917).

Bossu, Nicolas. *Nouveaux Voyages aux Indes Occidentales.* 2 vols., Amsterdam, 1769.

Boyd, Mark F. "The Fortifications at San Marcos de Apalache," *Florida Historical Society Quarterly*, XV, 3–34 (July, 1936).

Brannon, Peter A. "The Pensacola Indian Trade," *Florida Historical Society Quarterly*, XXXI, 1–15 (July, 1952).

Burson, Caroline Maude. *The Stewardship of Don Esteban Miró, 1782–1792*. New Orleans, American Printing Company, 1940.

Caughey, John Walton. "Alexander McGillivray and the Creek Crisis, 1783–1784," *New Spain and the Anglo-American West* (2 vols., Los Angeles, 1932), I, 263–288.

———. *Bernardo de Gálvez in Louisiana, 1776–1783*. Berkeley, University of California Press, 1934.

———. *McGillivray of the Creeks*. Norman, University of Oklahoma Press, 1938.

Corbitt, D. C. "Papers Relating to the Georgia-Florida Frontier, 1784–1800," *Georgia Historical Quarterly*, XX, 356–365; XXI, 73–83, 185–188, 274–293, 373–381; XXII, 72–76, 184–191, 286–291, 391–394; XXIII, 77–79, 189–202, 300–303, 381–387, XXIV, 77–83, 150–157, 257–271, 374–381; XXV, 67–76, 159–171 (1936–1941).

Cox, Isaac Joslin. *The West Florida Controversy, 1798–1813*. Baltimore, Johns Hopkins Press, 1918.

Dictionary of American Biography.

Dictionary of National Biography.

Dobie, J. Frank. *The Mustangs*. Boston, Houghton Mifflin Company, 1952.

Downes, Randolph G. "Creek-American Relations, 1782–1790," *Georgia Historical Quarterly*, XXI, 142–184 (June, 1937).

Ellicott, Andrew. *The Journal of Andrew Ellicott, 1796–1800*. Philadelphia, 1803.

The Favrot Papers, 1695–1812. New Orleans, Louisiana State Museum, 1940.

Gatschet, Albert S. "The Migration Legend of the Kasi'tha Tribe," *Transactions of the Academy of Science of St. Louis,* V, 33–101 (1886–91).

Gazette de France, 10 Thermidor, An X.

Goff, John H. "The Path to Oakfuskee; Upper Trading Route in Georgia to the Creek Indians," *Georgia Historical Quarterly,* XXXIX, 1–36, 152–171 (March, June, 1955).

Greenslade, Marie Taylor (Mrs. John W.). "A Journal of John Forbes, May, 1803. The Seizure of William Augustus Bowles," *Florida Historical Society Quarterly,* IX, 279–289 (April, 1931).

———. "William Panton," *Florida Historical Society Quarterly,* XIV, 107–129 (October, 1935).

Hamilton, Peter J. *Colonial Mobile.* Boston, Houghton Mifflin Company, 1898.

Haskins, Charles H. "The Yazoo Land Companies," *American Historical Association Papers,* V, 395–437 (1891).

Hawkins, Benjamin. *Letters of Benjamin Hawkins, 1796–1806. Georgia Historical Society Collections,* Vol. IX (1916)

———. *A Sketch of the Creek Country, in the Years 1798 and 1799. Georgia Historical Society Collections,* Vol. III, Part I (1848).

Hill, Roscoe R. *Descriptive Catalogue of the Documents relating to the History of the United States in the Papeles Procedentes de Cuba deposited in the Archivo General de Indias at Seville.* Washington, Carnegie Institution, 1916.

Hodge, Frederick Webb. *Handbook of American Indians North of Mexico. Bureau of American Ethnology Bulletin 30.* 2 vols., Washington, 1912.

Hooker, Richard J. (ed.). *The Carolina Backcountry on the Eve of the Revolution—the Diary of Charles Woodmason.* Chapel Hill, The University of North Carolina Press, 1953.

Houck, Louis. *The Spanish Régime in Missouri.* 2 vols., Chicago, 1909.

Humphreys, Frank L. *Life of David Humphreys.* 2 vols., New York, 1917.

Hutchins, Thomas. *An Historical Narrative and Topographical Description of Louisiana, and West-Florida.* Philadelphia, 1784.

Johnson, Cecil. *British West Florida, 1763–1783.* New Haven, Yale University Press, 1943.

Jones, Charles C., Jr. *The History of Georgia.* 2 vols., Boston, Houghton Mifflin Company, 1883.

Kinnaird, Lawrence. "International Rivalry in the Creek Country. Part I, The Ascendancy of Alexander McGillivray, 1783–1789," *Florida Historical Society Quarterly,* X, 59–85 (October, 1931).

———. "The Significance of William Augustus Bowles' Seizure of Panton's Apalachee Store in 1792," *Florida Historical Society Quarterly,* IX, 156–192 (January, 1931).

———. *Spain in the Mississippi Valley, 1765–1794. Translations of Materials from the Spanish Archives in the Bancroft Library. American Historical Association Annual Report for 1945,* 3 vols., Washington, 1946, 1949.

Le Page du Pratz, ———. *Histoire de la Louisiane.* 3 vols., Paris, 1758.

McAlister, Lyle N. "The Marine Forces of William Augustus Bowles and his State of Muskogee," *Florida Historical Society Quarterly,* XXXII, 3–27 (July, 1953).

McDermott, John Francis. *A Glossary of Mississippi*

Valley French, 1673–1850. St. Louis, Washington University Studies, 1941.

Michaud. *Biographie Universelle*. Paris, n.d.

Milfort, (Louis). *Mémoire ou Coup-d'oeil Rapide sur mes Différens voyages et mon Séjour dans la Nation Crëck. Par le Gal. Milfort, Tastanégy ou Grand Chef de Guerre de la Nation Crëck, et Général de Brigade au Service de la République Française*. Paris, an XI—(1802).

Peters, Richard. *Treaties between the United States and the Indian Tribes*. Boston, 1848.

Pickett, Albert James. *History of Alabama, and Incidentally of Georgia and Mississippi, from the Earliest Period*. 2 vols., Charleston, 1851.

Pope, John. *A Tour through the Southern and Western Territories of the United States of North-America; the Spanish Dominions on the River Mississippi, and the Floridas; the Countries of the Creek Nations; and many Uninhabited Parts*. New edition, New York, 1888.

Robertson, James Alexander. *Louisiana under the Rule of Spain, France, and the United States, 1785–1807*. 2 vols., Cleveland, Arthur H. Clark Company, 1911.

Roe, Frank Gilbert. *The Indian and his Horse*. Norman, The University of Oklahoma Press, 1955.

Romans, Bernard. *A Concise Natural History of East and West Florida*. New York, 1775.

Savelle, Max. *George Morgan, Colony Builder*. New York, Columbia University Press, 1932.

Shaw, Helen Leonard. *British Administration of the Southern Indians, 1756–1783*. Lancaster, 1931.

State Papers and Correspondence Bearing upon the Purchase of the Territory of Louisiana. 57th Congress, 2nd Session, House of Representatives Document 431 (Washington, 1903).

Surrey, N. M. Miller. *Calendar of Manuscripts in Paris Archives and Libraries Relating to the History of the Mississippi Valley to 1803.* 2 vols., Washington, Carnegie Institution, 1928.

Swan, Caleb. "Position and State of Manners and Arts in the Creek, or Muscogee Nation in 1791," in H. R. Schoolcraft, *Information Respecting the History, Condition and Prospects of the Indian Tribes of the United States* (5 vols., Philadelphia, 1855), V, 251–283.

Swanton, John R. *Early History of the Creek Indians and their Neighbors. Bureau of American Ethnology Bulletin No. 73,* Washington, 1922.

———. *The Indians of the Southeastern United States. Bureau of American Ethnology Bulletin No. 137.* Washington, 1946.

———. "Religious Beliefs and Medical Practices of the Creek Indians," *Forty-second Annual Report of the Bureau of American Ethnology, 1924–25,* pp. 473–672. Washington, 1928.

———. "Social Organization and Social Usages of the Indians of the Creek Confederacy," *Forty-second Annual Report of the Bureau of American Ethnology, 1924–25,* pp. 23–472. Washington, 1928.

———. *Source Material on the History and Ethnology of the Caddo Indians. Bureau of American Ethnology Bulletin 132.* Washington, 1942.

———. *Source Material for the Social and Ceremonial Life of the Choctaw Indians. Bureau of American Ethnology Bulletin 103.* Washington, 1931.

Tarvin, Marion Elisha. "The Muscogees or Creek Indians 1519 to 1893," *Alabama Historical Quarterly,* XVII, 125–145 (Fall, 1955).

Trumbull, John. *Autobiography.* Edited by Theodore Suzer. New Haven, Yale University Press, 1953.

Turner, Frederick J. "The Policy of France toward the Mississippi Valley in the period of Washington and Adams," *American Historical Review,* X, 249–279 (January, 1905).

Whitaker, Arthur Preston. "Alexander McGillivray," *North Carolina Historical Review,* V, 181–203, 289–309 (April, July, 1928).

———. *The Mississippi Question, 1795–1803.* New York, Appleton-Century, 1934.

———. "The South Carolina Yazoo Company," *Mississippi Valley Historical Review,* XVI, 383–394 (December, 1929).

———. *The Spanish-American Frontier, 1783–1795: the Westward Movement and the Spanish Retreat in the Mississippi Valley.* Boston, Houghton Mifflin, 1927.

Index

INDEX

ABENAKI Indians (Owabenaki), location of, 108, 108 n.

Abihka Indians, village of, 188, 188 n.

Acadians, Milford claims were at New Madrid, xxix, 73–74; discussed by editor, 74 n.

Adair, James, tells composition of war medicine, 171 n; says several nations live with Creeks, 183 n; describes customs of Chickasaw widows, 198 n.

Alabama River, 182 n; Alibamu Indians located on, 183.

Alibamu Indians, kill Creeks, 165; pursued by Creeks, 165, 177–82; protected by French, 182–83; unite with Creeks, 183–84.

Altamaha River, 9, 10 n.

André, Major John, captured, 127.

Anglo-Americans, criticized by Milford, xlvii, 7, 8, 22, 49–52, 56–57, 58–59, 79, 89, 90–92, 137, 218–19.

Apalachee Indians, location of, 194 n; remnant merged with Creeks, 194 n; not identical with Seminoles, 195 n.

Apalachicola Indians, Spanish priests among, 191–93; Milford confuses with Seminoles, 194, 195 n; location of, 194 n.

Arkansas (Quapaw) Indians, encountered by Milford, 65, 68.

Arnold, Benedict, 127 n; betrays U.S., 126–27.

Artaguiette, Diron d', defeated by Chickasaws and Natchez, 187 n.

Atakapa Indians, Milford visits, 61–63; meaning of name, 62, 62n.

Augusta (Georgia), growth of, 5, 5 n, 131.

BALIZE (Balise) Post, 55, 55 n.

Bartram, William, cited regarding Augusta, 5 n; describes plantation of de St. Pierre, 6 n; Mobile, 38 n; Creek council house, 146 n; denies Creeks burned captives, 154 n; describes Creek standard, 156 n.

The Lakeside Classics